YOUNG BLOOD

YOUNG BLOOD

Juvenile Justice and the Death Penalty

Edited By

Shirley Dicks

 Prometheus Books

59 John Glenn Drive
Amherst, NewYork 14228-2197

Published 1995 by Prometheus Books

99 98 97 96 95   5 4 3 2 1

Library of Congress Cataloging-in-Publication Data

Young blood : juvenile justice and the death penalty / [edited] by
    Shirley Dicks.
        p.   cm.
    Includes bibliographical references.
    ISBN 0–87975–953–4 (alk. paper)
    1. Juvenile justice, Administration of—United States—Case
studies. 2. Juvenile delinquency—United States—Case studies.
3. Capital punishment—United States—Case studies. 4. Death
row inmates—United States—Case studies. I. Dicks, Shirley,
1940–   .
HV9104.Y66   1995
364.6'6'0835—dc20   95–6336
                                                                      CIP

Printed in the United States of America on acid-free paper.

This book is dedicated to my youngest daughter, Maria Mathews, who I adopted when she was born, in the hopes that she will never find herself in trouble. She has been my lifesaver the past few years as I fight to save her father, my son, from death row.

Contents

Part One: Experts and Concerned Citizens

7

Part Two: Juveniles and the Death Penalty

Part Three: Families

Part Four: Programs and Organizations

Conclusion

PART ONE

EXPERTS AND CONCERNED CITIZENS

1

Should Teens Be Tried as Adults?*

Ron Harris

A Nation's Children in Lockup

In separate cases three years ago, Michael Harris and Walter Biggs, both of Los Angeles, were arrested and charged with robbery. Both Harris and Biggs (whose real names are not used here) were convicted and sentenced to custody. Harris, sixteen, served two and a half years; Biggs, twenty-five, however, did only eighteen months.

It wasn't that Harris was the more dangerous criminal, nor was the difference merely one of the vagaries of the justice system. Harris did more time because, as a juvenile, he was sentenced to the California Youth Authority, while Biggs was sent to a state prison.

"That's not uncommon," one Los Angeles juvenile parole

---

*Ron Harris is a staff writer for the *Los Angeles Times*. Originally printed in the *Los Angeles Times,* August 22, 23, 24, and 25, 1993. Copyright, 1993, *Los Angeles Times*. Reprinted by permission.

officer said. "Juveniles sent to the Youth Authority normally serve longer sentences than adults in state prison."

Such is the rougher, tougher world of juvenile justice.

It is a world where some states lock up larger percentages of children than adults, where youngsters who are traditionally denied jury trials may serve longer sentences than their adult counterparts, where youths are often housed in overcrowded facilities and sometimes punished in ways that would be unthinkable in state prisons.

All because people believed something that wasn't true.

Beginning about 1975, crimes by children in the United States began a steady decline, but the public perception was that juvenile delinquency was going through the roof.

So the United States began to lock up its wayward youngsters at unprecedented rates, eventually transforming the way the nation deals with them.

Once, juvenile crime brought determined attempts to rehabilitate kids, even though that sometimes required keeping them in custody.

Today, virtually all authorities on juvenile justice agree, custody has become largely an end in itself. The pendulum has swung away from rehabilitation and toward punishment.

Recent juvenile crime statistics make it increasingly clear that it has not worked.

Starting in the mid-1970s, the experts say, America decided to get tough with its juvenile delinquents and to separate them from the rest of society, even though Justice Department figures showed juvenile crime declining. From 1978 to 1988, while the per capita rate of crime among youths dropped by 19 percent, their lockup rate increased by nearly 50 percent.

"The public got tough-minded, and the elected officials got tough-minded for them," said Fred Jordan, director of probation for San Francisco County. "We had a series of attorneys general who talked about the 'juvenile crime wave,' even though the numbers weren't going up."

Until this shift began, juvenile court had functioned as society's stern surrogate parent; the court's role was to bolster family discipline—or to provide discipline where there was none—by applying an additional measure of control and guidance for wayward children.

Children who committed crimes, the court reasoned, were not hardened criminals, but still-forming youngsters who often could be put back on track; they could be admonished, or counseled, or moved from dysfunctional homes to structured, nurturing environments. The court was there to protect and to guide them, not to punish.

But in the tough-minded '70s and '80s, rehabilitation took a back seat. States passed laws calling for more and longer incarceration of the young, and when punishment inside juvenile facilities was deemed too soft, the states enacted measures allowing thousands of children to be tried and sentenced as adults.

Few inside the juvenile-justice system believed that longer, stiffer sentences would rehabilitate children. In fact, studies in California show a correlation between longer sentences and how often minors return to crime. The public, however, wanted retribution, and many voices argued that as long as kids were in custody, at least they couldn't cause more trouble.

Increasingly, as children were locked up in large, prisonlike juvenile halls, youth camps, and training schools, the facilities became overcrowded—breeding grounds for abuse and violence.

"The juvenile code now is a punishment model," said Jerome Wasom, director of the Washington state Division of Juvenile Rehabilitation. "There's a much greater emphasis on sending kids to state institutions."

But, despite the harsher penalties, something happened four years ago that caught juvenile officials off guard: The rate of serious crimes among the nation's children and youths actually began to rise.

In 1991, the most recent year for which figures are available, juvenile homicides, forcible rapes, robberies, and aggravated assaults climbed to their highest levels in the nation's history. Although there were still fewer offenses of all kinds per capita than there were ten years earlier, the upsurge in more violent offenses has caused many in the juvenile-justice system to ask what has gone wrong.

Former U.S. Attorney General William P. Barr says the increases "clearly show that we must enact wholesale reform of the juvenile-justice system so that, for the vast majority of juvenile offenders, their first brush with the law is their last. But the long-term solution falls largely outside of law enforcement. It requires strengthening those basic institutions—family, schools, religious institutions, community groups—that are responsible for instilling values and creating law-abiding citizens."

Paradoxically—because it was assumed that the role of the juvenile court was to rehabilitate and to assist those who came before it—safeguards that the justice system guarantees adults were not afforded to children. Such safeguards were considered unnecessary or undesirable.

Children in juvenile court, for instance, do not have the right to a jury trial, nor, in most states, are they allowed bail. To "protect the reputation of children," proceedings in juvenile court are closed to the public and the press.

Even the terminology of juvenile court is different—designed, officials say, to spare children the taint of criminal proceedings.

Holding facilities for children prior to court appearances—the equivalent of adult jails—are called "detention." Instead of find-ings of guilt or innocence, juvenile courts reach a "disposition" for juvenile offenders. Youngsters are not "sentenced" but "placed."

"The idea was that you were going to treat these kids," said Robert Walker, a family law attorney in San Francisco who handles cases in juvenile court. "The children were going to get the services they needed." But now, he says, "although the ter-minology remains the same, the court has become much more like a mini-criminal court."

These days the terms serve as mere euphemisms, said John O'Toole, director of the National Center for Youth Law in San Francisco. "The justification in the past was that what was going to happen to you as a child was not going to be bad," he says. "That's just not true anymore. Kids are being punished, and they are being punished very harshly."

In the late 1970s, states began to amend juvenile codes, often going so far as to write the word "punishment" into sen-tencing guidelines.

Now, according to the Justice Department, on any given day, about one hundred thousand juveniles nationwide are in lockup—nearly a fifth of them in California.

As incarceration was mandated for specific offenses, dis-cretion was increasingly taken out of the hands of juvenile-court judges.

Consequently, many judges say they find themselves strait-jacketed, like Seattle Judge Norma Huggins, who says she sen-tenced one fifteen-year-old to two years in a state juvenile prison "because I had no choice."

"There was an outcry that children who are accused of crime need to get the same thing that adults get," said Huggins, who now handles adult cases. "But there is a difference. I see people every day who are professional criminals, who intend to live their lives taking advantage of other people. I don't think I can say that of a fifteen-year-old, that he's made up his mind to be a professional thief or a professional killer."

Adding to the punishment side of the ledger, many states rewrote laws so that more juveniles could be tried as adults. The result is that thousands are sent to adult prisons.

In New York, any juvenile sixteen or older accused of committing a crime is automatically transferred to adult court and, if found guilty, sentenced to an adult facility. In Florida, about six thousand juveniles are transferred to adult court each year at the sole discretion of the prosecuting attorney. In Illinois and Mississippi, any youth thirteen or older can be tried as an adult for any crime. In seventeen states, children as young as fourteen can be tried in adult court.

In California, the legislature in 1977 passed provisions so that, under a handful of serious charges such as murder, voluntary manslaughter, and armed robbery, children sixteen and older could be tried as adults. Each year, however, the list lengthened. Today it has grown to twenty-four offenses.

"Politicians keep beating their breasts wanting more and more punishment," said Michael Mahoney, former director of a maximum-security Illinois Youth Center and now executive director of a prison watchdog group in Joliet, Illinois. "They seize upon some crime that has caught the public eye. Then, they pass a law to make the punishment tougher, and the public nods its approval.

"I'm not arguing that there aren't some bad kids out there who need to be separated, but I think we have overdone it. I've seen thugs, and I've seen sixteen-year-olds who are lost, mixed-up kids. This whole idea of pushing kids into the adult system belies the fact there's a large disparity in criminality, maturity, and mental stability."

Juvenile-justice officials say that as the nation moved toward punishment, services that nurture children, bolster families, or intervene to keep kids out of trouble began to diminish. Now, they say, issues that could or should have been resolved earlier are ending up in juvenile court.

"There aren't enough community resources to deal with a lot of problems," said Juvenile Court Judge Sherman Smith in San Francisco. "We should have better recreational systems. Police officers should have more positive interaction with the community. We need better schools. These are the kinds of things we should do. [But now] the court is the primary source of intervention when it comes to children. The court should not be part of the front-end process. The court should be the last resort."

In the juvenile-justice system, probation officers have long been a force to help delinquent kids get their lives back on track. The probation officers' job is to watch over children, monitor their school performance, talk with their instructors, visit their homes, counsel them, review their progress, and recommend action.

Over the last fifteen years, however, probation departments have seen their budgets slashed and their role changed as the numbers of youngsters assigned to each officer have soared. Like teachers in overcrowded classrooms, the probation officers have seen their effectiveness diminish.

In Chicago, Cook County probation officer Angela Pierce struggles to keep track of sixty troubled juveniles from the impoverished Inglewood community. She sees each of them once a month.

"I'm just scratching the surface," she said. "These kids need a lot more than I can give them."

In Los Angeles, county probation officer Lisa Cunningham

said she envies Pierce. Her caseload is nearly two hundred children. "I wanted to be a probation officer to help people, but I have so many people who need the help that I don't have time to give them the attention they need," she said.

These days, juvenile-court officials say, if minors stay out of trouble, they do so mostly on their own. If they commit another offense, it is usually because the forces that first got them into trouble still exist.

"I had one kid who kept violating his probation," Chicago Juvenile Court Judge Charles May said.

> As a part of his probation, he was supposed to be at home at night by a certain time, but he would always miss his curfew. So, he's back in court and I tell him that I'm going to have to put him in detention for thirty days.
>
> He says, "Your honor, I just can't stay at home and watch my father beat up my mother." Now what am I supposed to do? I can't let this kid continue to skip curfew and violate a direct court order. He's got to go home. But am I supposed to force him into a house where a father is abusing a mother?

Many of the nation's juvenile-court judges face a similar quandary—a stream of delinquent children with a horde of contributing problems, and few answers other than incarceration.

"In Pennsylvania, we sometimes cannot come up with the services for kids to stay at home, and because we cannot, we'll put them in jail," said Naomi Post, whose job as director of the Philadelphia juvenile court's Restitution and Resource Planning Unit is to find the most suitable placement for delinquent children. "We can't just leave the child at home where he or she is not getting any help."

"Locking up a kid and giving that kid some structure is a

valid rehabilitation tool," said Judge Smith in San Francisco. "Just because you lock a kid up doesn't mean it's necessarily something negative. You're providing structure to show kids what to do right."

In nearly every state, judges and juvenile-court officials can point to model training schools where delinquent children have turned their lives around. But they admit such facilities are the exception.

Many of today's juvenile facilities have become overcrowded, often dangerous, sometimes brutal places where children sleep on floors, join gangs for their own protection, and receive harsh, sometimes abusive, treatment by those who watch over them.

In Seattle, detention supervisor Ed Woodley described one facility as a "school for crime"; in Pennsylvania, Post said she "wouldn't send a dog to Cromwell Heights," one of the state's facilities for juveniles.

Because of a shortage of facilities children who commit minor offenses often find themselves mixed in with tougher youths, said James Bell, staff attorney for the Youth Law Center in San Francisco.

There have been many stories of abuses inside juvenile facilities. In Florida, until a court order ended such practices in 1988, ten-year-olds sent to reform school for petty thievery were hogtied and thrown into strip-cell isolation, sometimes for as long as sixty days. In Oklahoma, prior to a court settlement in 1985, children were placed in straitjackets and put in isolation. In Idaho, thirteen- and fourteen-year-olds were "given the standing wall," in which they stood with noses pressed against the wall for as long as sixteen hours a day for such infractions as talking.

In Arizona, children were handcuffed naked to beds or had

their feet and hands handcuffed to the four corners of their bunk. In New Orleans, juvenile offenders complain that they are routinely beaten by sheriff's deputies at the local detention center.

"We're talking about kinds of physical and mental punishment that don't go on even in adult institutions," said David Lambert, an attorney for the Youth Law Center, which has filed and won numerous cases regarding the treatment of juveniles in state facilities.

"Kids need to be held accountable, but not by punishing them by putting them in a brutal, dehumanizing institution for six to eight months, where they continually learn to survive by intimidating other people, where they lose more respect for authority, which, in turn, increases the odds that when they are released from that institution they are going to engage in similar or worse criminal activity," he said.

It is clear, say those who monitor the juvenile-court system, that more and longer incarceration does not appear to be working. As the incarceration rate has gone up, so has the percentage of juveniles who are rearrested for crimes after their release.

"The way the system is set up now, they're coming out worse than when they went in," said Lambert of the Youth Law Center. "They come out embittered, hardened."

Consequently, some states are beginning to reevaluate the way they handle children, and are seeking more cost-effective methods.

Currently, the nation is spending more than $3.2 billion annually to keep children in custody, and the annual price tag for one youngster's incarceration averages more than $30,000.

"The amount of money we're spending on them, we could almost pay them to stay out of trouble," said Dan MacAllair of the Center for Juvenile and Criminal Justice in San Francisco.

"I mean, that's more than a year's tuition to Stanford or Harvard."

Increasingly, juvenile-justice officials themselves have begun to see an overriding correlation between juvenile delinquency and such factors as poverty, physical and emotional abuse, neglect, family dysfunction, and educational deficiencies. Consequently, many have concluded that just locking up youths is not the answer.

In Philadelphia, presiding Juvenile Court Judge Frank Reynolds says that "until you deal positively with these children, particularly those of the urban poor, you're going to suffer. The less time and energy a city spends on those children, the more miserable a city will become. If the major cities of this country do not begin to grasp that as an ever-present reality, their communities will continue to decline."

Gregory's File: A Childhood of Neglect, a Life of Crime

As seventeen-year-old Gregory stood before her, charged with drug dealing, King County Superior Court Judge Norma Huggins studied his juvenile record and came to the conclusion that she had reached in so many other cases.

"This kid never even had a chance," she told herself.

Gregory's file was filled with ominous details—gang membership, car theft, weapon possession.

But it was filled, too, with evidence that life had stacked the deck against him almost from birth—with abandonment, abuse, poverty, and neglect.

To Huggins, it seemed that Gregory had been almost destined for this day when a judge would be trying to protect the community from him while at the same time trying to rescue him from the forces that had shaped him.

Cases like Gregory's have become a focal point in the country's juvenile-justice system, officials say, because while policies have been tailored to deal with hardened, heartless juvenile offenders, most of the youngsters filing through courtrooms and filling up juvenile prisons are, like Gregory, as much victims as villains.

While their crimes differ and their circumstances vary, officials say that most children being housed in the nation's juvenile facilities share one experience:

"Neglect," says Margaret Nickish of St. Gabriel's School, a suburban Philadelphia custody facility for delinquent boys. "It is the biggest common denominator among the children that we see."

Judges complain that even as they carry out the nation's mandate for tougher sentencing, they know that many of the juveniles they are sending to jail are not criminals by choice but the product of abuse, poverty, and inattention.

Often, they are children of impoverished, overwhelmed mothers and absentee fathers. Or they are raised by emotionally crippled, chemically dependent parents, by overmatched grandparents, uninterested aunts, uncles or cousins, or by brothers and sisters themselves barely removed from adolescence.

Left with Lockups

They are orphans and foster children, high school dropouts, academic underachievers for whom school holds little hope or relevance. Their childhoods have been one long descent through the nation's porous safety nets to juvenile court, historically the last and most intense stop in a series of rehabilitative efforts.

In today's juvenile system, however, punishment has moved to center stage. While rehabilitation is still regarded as a goal, public programs designed to offer poor children counseling and other support services have been choked off by a lack of funding.

Consequently, judges increasingly find themselves exercising the only option left: lock them up where they can do no harm and hope that something good will come of it.

So it was to be today for Gregory, whose last name is omitted, as required by juvenile court rules, but whose life offers a case study of many of the circumstances that deliver children to lockup.

Gregory was scarred almost from the beginning. Just before his first birthday, his father, a mentally disturbed and physically disabled Vietnam veteran, killed his mother, starting the boy down a path that would eventually land him in Huggins's courtroom.

Streetwise Childhood

While his father went to prison, Gregory and his older sister were shuffled to relatives in Seattle, then to Memphis. But their father was paroled five years later, and they were returned to him in Seattle.

There, although poor and often unkempt, they attended school and appeared to be no different from other children of six and eleven in the neighborhood. By night, however, they helped their father peddle marijuana up and down the city's back streets, usually falling asleep on a makeshift bed in the back of his van as he made the rounds.

"We would help him package it up," Gregory recalled. "At first, what we mostly did was get all the seeds out. Then he showed us how to weigh it on this scale he had so that you got just the right amount."

Gregory's father proved to be his own best customer, and as his drug and alcohol dependency grew, the family lost its home. For nearly four years, Gregory and his sister wandered with their father from homeless shelter to relative to acquaintance to motel to shelter.

When Gregory was nine, he and his sister were taken from their father and placed in separate foster homes. They would never live together again. Over the next four years, Gregory would alternate between foster homes and life with an alcoholic aunt who would tend to him for a few months, then be overwhelmed by the chore.

Gang as Family

And with each foster home there were new rules, new expectations, new people. Gregory became withdrawn, suppressing his real feelings in order to get along, and learning to tell adults what they wanted to hear, not what they needed to know.

At thirteen, he wandered into a neighborhood gang, which became his real family, protecting, consoling, and advising him. Its members taught him to fend for himself, to shoplift, to steal cars, to get guns.

"I just kind of got into it," Gregory says. "You don't join a gang because you want to do something bad. Sometimes you just need somebody to watch your back."

As his gang involvement increased, Gregory—until then a solid B student—began to skip school. His grades fell. His priorities shifted. Money became a near-obsession. "When I don't have money, I feel bad," he says. "It's like I'm nobody, nothing."

He began to sell drugs. With that role came money, status, and prestige. "Everywhere I went, people knew me," he said.

Eventually, the police came to know him too. Late one night, when he was again living with his aunt, officers burst into his bedroom and arrested him for auto theft and possession of a gun and drugs. He was fourteen.

After five weeks in detention, Gregory was found guilty, placed on probation, and returned to his aunt. But within six months he was arrested, again for auto theft.

He spent a year and two months in a lockup, then was transferred to a group home where he got psychiatric counseling. By now, his life had left its mark. Counselors noted that his emotional problems included severe depression, mood swings, insomnia, nightmares, low self-esteem, poor coping skills, and lack of self-control. They prescribed drugs.

Father Returns

Eventually, Gregory's father, who had remarried, returned and won a sixty-day trial custody.

"I didn't really want to live with my father," Gregory says. "I mean, I didn't know what to expect because he had never really taken care of me. . . . But I wanted to get out of that group home, and he is my father."

At sixteen, Gregory moved with his new stepmother and his unpredictable father into a small, two-bedroom apartment already occupied by a cousin, her husband, and their two children. The three made do on the father's disability check.

As a provision of Gregory's release, the court had ordered that he continue psychiatric counseling. He received none.

He attended a nearby school and started off well. Teachers reported him well mannered, well liked, and disciplined. Within weeks, according to his academic counselor, he had become a favorite tutor among students in the school's tutorial program.

That brief semblance of order ended quickly. Near the end of the second month, the cousin and her husband, tired of bickering with Gregory's parents, asked them to leave. Gregory stayed on, and his father promised to send money for his expenses. It never came. Gregory had no bus fare, nothing for lunch or school supplies. He secretly began selling small amounts of marijuana for an adult who lived nearby.

After three weeks, the cousin, angry at the father's failure to keep his promise, dropped Gregory and a cardboard box with his belongings on the doorstep of a dingy transient motel room that his father now called home. There was one bed. Gregory slept on the floor.

"I could see this pattern starting all over again with my father," Gregory said. So he began a desperate search. He thought about moving in with his sister, now a twenty-one-year-old welfare recipient who lived in a one-bedroom slum apartment with her two small children and a boyfriend, whom Gregory suspected of crack cocaine addiction. That wouldn't work. Just weeks earlier, he recalled, his sister had borrowed $40 that he had saved while in custody because she had run out of milk and diapers for the baby.

Finally, Gregory slipped out to a pay phone and called collect to the mother of a friend who had often offered her home if he needed a place to stay. It was cramped, but clean and comfortable. The family welcomed him, gave him his own room, doled out a weekly allowance.

But old habits die hard.

Six weeks later, Gregory was standing before Judge Huggins, accused of selling $100 worth of marijuana to an undercover police officer. While he awaited trial, neither his father, aunt, sister, nor any other relative visited him.

Judge Huggins looked at the balance sheet. In Gregory's favor were good grades and a letter of support from one instructor. Then came the other side of the ledger: No parent present. No other relatives available. Previous adults did not provide proper supervision. Third offense.

There were no alternatives. Gregory was sentenced to up to three years in custody.

Cases like Gregory's stream through the nation's juvenile courts in an unending procession, and as a result, many justice officials say, the nation's juvenile custody facilities have in large part become holding pens for disadvantaged children.

"We're getting more and more youngsters who are very emotionally upset, youngsters who need a lot more attention and counseling than in previous years," says Nickish of the suburban Philadelphia school for delinquent boys. "The problems are different out there. Many, many times after reading the records, I say to myself, 'Thank God I didn't have to grow up in these days.'"

Rising Tensions

A study of fifteen-year-olds in custody in New York City, for example, found that 75 percent were from single-parent homes and 35 percent read at fourth-grade level or below. Social workers say that many of these children feel locked outside, almost as removed from American society as foreigners observing America on television. Internal and external pressures have heightened tensions in their homes to a flash point, and as they venture into neighborhoods devoid of recreational activities and services, there is little release.

For some, poverty is so intense and the community so oppressive that being in jail is actually better than being at home, juvenile court officials say. "It strikes you kind of odd on its face," says Fred Davis, head of a five-hundred-bed juvenile detention facility in Chicago.

> But if you're in a gang environment, there's shooting constantly in the neighborhood, there's dope all over the neighborhood. You could be shot or killed. There's usually just the mother trying to grapple with all these children. You're living in a raggedy, roach-infested apartment, sleeping four to a bed.
>
> In detention, you're in a place that's clean, it's safe, it's quiet, there's order, you have your own room, your own bed. I know it sounds crazy, but that's the reality for some of these kids. I mean, I've actually had kids tell me that being here was better than being at home.

Ultimately, as America's intercity children take on the characteristics of the circumstances in which they live, they regurgitate their daily diet of pain, uncertainty, violence, and abuse in delinquent behavior.

"If a child has been raised in a house where different men are coming and going, mother is drinking during the day, often leaving the child to fend for himself, the child having to deal with neighbors in a violence-torn community, that's the only norm the child knows," says Dr. John Griffith, director of clinical services at Kenren Mental Health Center in South-Central Los Angeles.

"Someone born into that neighborhood, with that kind of conditioning—his perception of the world would be anxiety-provoking and hostile. That child feels he has to defend and protect himself."

A Familiar Cycle

Cary Quashen, who counsels juveniles at Avalon Treatment Program in North Hollywood, says:

> I'm working with a fourteen-year-old girl whose dad was killed by police in a robbery before she was born, and her mother has been a drug addict all her life. So the kid is being raised by her grandmother. The mom goes to prison for prostitution and cocaine, and when she gets out she moves in with the grandmother, where she is staying in the same room as her daughter.
>
> The mother is still getting loaded, bringing in all kinds of men, disappearing for days at a time, hiding drugs in the kid's clothes. The kid is watching all of this. So the kid starts running away, stealing and getting loaded.
>
> Now she's committed a crime, but really what she's doing is acting out her pain at home. She's a victim of circumstances. That doesn't give her the excuse to do what she's doing, but that's why she's doing it.

Judge Walter Williams said that the relationship between neglect, abuse, and delinquency became crystal clear to him when, after ten years of handling cases of child abuse and neglect in Chicago's Juvenile Dependency Court, he moved last year to delinquency court.

"Many of the kids that I was seeing over there as abused and neglected kids, I'm seeing over here now as delinquent kids charged with crimes," Williams says, "I mean the exact same kids."

When those children come to court in a criminal case, however, the abuse and neglect seldom have relevance to what happens to them.

A Hamstrung System

"Sometimes our system fails these children," says Naomi M. Post, whose job it is to find the most suitable placements for many of Philadelphia's juvenile offenders.

"When we get a kid on the delinquent side, we deal with him strictly on that. It doesn't matter that the child has these dependent issues that may be influencing his behavior. This is one of the problems that the system has failed to recognize for years. We didn't understand that family dysfunction played a major role in the behavior of these children."

Orville Armstrong, presiding juvenile judge in Los Angeles East Lake Division, describes the frustration he experiences every time that he reviews a progress report before deciding whether to release a youngster he has sentenced to a stint at one of Los Angeles County's youth camps.

The report will usually read something like this: In the first weeks or so, the kid was uncooperative and showed no progress. In the next few weeks, he still had problems but showed signs of improvement. In the third month, he was really doing well, his grades had picked up, he was beginning to be more involved. By the end, he is just great, he's an active leader among the boys, he's making exceptional grades. He's really cleaned up his act and is dong wonderful things.

So, he's standing before me in court and I'm getting ready to release this kid and I will give him a lecture. I tell him how he has really improved, how he should be proud of his accomplishments. I talk about how he has laid down this strong foundation on which to go forward and build a strong, productive future.

And even as the last words trail off my lips, I know that

in all likelihood he'll be back, because we're sending him back to the same environment, the same structure, the same streets, that got him here in the first place.

Nationally, an estimated seven in ten children who are placed in long-term custody will be back, juvenile delinquency officials say. Consequently, many officials have begun to question the nation's emphasis on simply putting, without additional therapy, children where they can do no harm for the moment.

"Right now we're just simply punishing kids," says Huggins, the judge who sentenced Gregory. "We are addressing their delinquent behavior, but we are not addressing the problems that spawned these children, the same problems we are going to send them back to when they are out of custody."

Hand of Punishment Falls Heavily on Black Youths

The statistics are so startling that they appear to cry out for an explanation:

Seventy percent of juveniles who are arrested nationally for criminal offenses are white, yet whites make up only 35 percent of those in custody. Black juveniles make up only about 25 percent of those arrested, but 44 percent of those in custody.

Out of every 100,000 white youngsters in the nation 287 are in custody, but for every 100,000 black youngsters 1,009 are in custody.

To some inside the juvenile justice system, these figures from 1991, the latest available, present a disparity that smacks of racism and bias.

But the numbers are not that easily explained. Prosecutors

and police say there is a good reason for the gap: Black juveniles are arrested for a disproportionate number of serious and violent offenses, which carry tougher sentences. Law enforcement officials say that explains the inordinate number of African-Americans in the nation's juvenile halls, training schools, youth camps, and state correctional facilities.

There is some truth to that explanation. For some offenses, FBI statistics show, black juveniles are arrested at two, three, and sometimes even five times the rate of their white counterparts. However, given those rates in total, white juveniles still outnumber black juveniles arrested for murder, rape, aggravated assault, burglary, and drug offenses.

On the other side of the analysis, many public defenders, parents, and even some judges blame the disparity on a juvenile-justice system dominated by biased, insensitive white judges and prosecutors who release white youths to probation or treatment programs for the same offenses that send black youths into custody.

Again, there is evidence to support their claim. Justice Department statistics, they note, show that black juveniles receive stiffer terms for drug offenses, motor vehicle theft, and burglary than whites charged with the same crimes.

But how do these cities account for separate studies in Missouri and Pennsylvania showing that black judges are more likely than white judges to place black juveniles in custody?

While each claim has some merit, the punishment gap between white and black children also appears to reflect a larger and harsher reality, one rooted in the nation's changed attitude about how to deal with the children of poor and disadvantaged families.

During the last decade, juvenile-justice officials say, the nation moved away from social programs designed to aid indigent children.

"The people in this country, having destroyed the children of poor people through neglect, have decided that they are not going to do anything to repair the damage." said Judge Frank Reynolds, Philadelphia's presiding juvenile-court justice. "The alternative then is to just lock them up. And that's what they are doing."

Across the country, states and counties have largely abandoned rehabilitation efforts for juveniles as the public has called for punishment through time in lockup.

One result is that the faces of those inside the juvenile-detention facilities have changed. Eight years ago, most were white. Now most are black, and, in any case, most of the juveniles in custody are poor and undereducated.

(Because of reporting disparities, figures for Latino juveniles are impossible to pin down accurately, but in California, according to a study by the National Council on Crime and Delinquency, Latino youngsters generally appear to be incarcerated at a rate roughly matching their percentage of the population.)

Opportunity Is the Key

Juvenile-justice officials say there are two underlying reasons for the change inside juvenile halls.

• Children with more opportunities—such as good schools, recreation, supportive community organizations, involved churches, and stable families—end up in court less often.

"Delinquency and lack of opportunity are two things that go together," said Robert Walavich, head of probation for suburban Chicago areas. "Opportunities can mean an end to delinquency for a kid because he's less likely to get into trouble in the first place."

• When children do get into trouble, those who do not have working parents, supportive school officials, readily available counseling facilities, and support organizations are much more likely to be placed in custody.

Consequently, just as black children make up a disproportionate share of the children mired in poverty, of those trapped in dysfunctional families, of high school students who drop out or are expelled, of those living in desolate urban neighborhoods, so do they bear the brunt of get-tough policies toward juveniles.

Perhaps the best example of the change that has taken place in the complexion of the juvenile custody population can be seen in the nation's response to youths involved with drugs.

Analysts say that though murder and robbery make for bigger headlines, drug crimes are responsible for vastly higher numbers of juvenile arrests and incarcerations.

From 1968 to 1981, according to FBI statistics, the per capita arrest rate for black juveniles lagged behind that of whites for drug violations. Between 1982 and 1984, however, the arrest rate for blacks moved just ahead.

In 1985, the numbers exploded; arrests of black youths for drug-related offenses skyrocketed. Paradoxically, white-youth arrest rates during the same period fell significantly—22 percent—even though federal agencies reported that the drug *use* rate by white youngsters was actually higher than that by black youths.

That increase in arrests, however, appears to be only the first factor in the dramatic rise in the number of black youngsters in custody. The second, and more important, factor is what happens to those juveniles once they come to court.

Despite the disparity in arrest rates, the total number of white juveniles brought to court on drug charges in 1990 exceeded the total number of blacks by 6,300. As those cases were sifted through the juvenile-court system, however, a far greater number of white youths were sent home without being tried, were released to drug counseling programs, or were placed on probation. Consequently, 2,200 more blacks than whites ended up in correctional facilities.

The disparity is even greater for violent crimes. In 1990, 32,200 more white juveniles than black juveniles were arrested for crimes such as murder, forcible rape, robbery and assault, and aggravated assault. Despite that difference, 300 more blacks than whites were placed in custody, and 2,100 more blacks than whites were transferred out of juvenile court so they could be tried in more punitive adult courts.

Disparity on Display

Across the nation, this disparity is played out in almost every category of offense.

In Chicago, for example, studies show that youngsters from the predominately black South Side and West Side neighborhoods who were charged with property offenses, such as minor theft, were twice as likely to be brought to trial as youngsters from the predominantly white North Side.

In California, according to a 1992 study by the National Council on Crime and Delinquency, black delinquents were four times more likely than whites to be committed to the California Youth Authority, the juvenile equivalent of prison, whether it was the first offense or the third.

Black youngsters were twice as likely as whites to be incarcerated for a serious property or sex offense, three times more likely for a violent offense, seven times more likely for a serious drug offense, and nearly ten times more likely for a serious weapons offense.

"After you control for violence of offense, you still find that black kids were more likely to be committed to the California Youth Authority than white kids who committed similar crimes," said David Steinhard, who directed the study.

Consequently, while blacks make up only 9 percent of the state's youth population, they account for 34 percent of youngsters in secure-custody facilities.

The reasons for disparities in custody rates are numerous, juvenile-justice officials and analysts say; race is a factor, class is a factor, severity and number of offenses are factors.

Ultimately, however, they say that what happens to children involved in delinquent activity comes down to the availability of resources.

"The whole thing really addresses resources for kids even before they start coming into the system," said Raul Solis, chief of juvenile field services for the Los Angeles County Probation Department.

> That's why we've been concentrating on going after young kids, at-risk kids, the younger brothers of gang members before they get into trouble. That's where it's at in our opinion.
>
> These kids are very isolated from access to things that most people take for granted every day. They see this mainstream on television, and their existence is very different. Many of them have never even been to a restaurant. They've never ordered from a menu. Some of these kids have never seen the ocean. Many of them have never learned how to swim because they never had the opportunity.
>
> All of the things other kids get exposure to, these kids don't have. But because of dwindling resources, we must deal with those kids who are arrested, and we have less money and personnel to deal with kids before they get into the system.

Once a crime is committed, it is often a slippery slope into a correctional facility for those without outside assistance.

"If a kid is picked up in the suburbs, depending on the crime, the chances are, if he's got the resources available, the kid won't hit the front door of the courtroom," Walavich said.

When children of the middle- and upper-class do come to court, they often arrive with both parents in tow, community counselors at their side, school representatives bearing report cards, and private attorneys presenting their cases.

"You have some excellent lawyers in the public defender's office, but they do get overwhelmed," Solis said. "I'm not so sure that kids aren't getting short shrift because of that.

Chicago Juvenile Judge Charles May is sure.

"Kids represented by private attorneys are usually much better off," he said. "That has a tremendous influence. The public attorneys do a good job, but in too many cases they just shoot from the hip. Good lawyers come up with the proposals. Ordinary lawyers, whom most black and poor kids get, just stand there."

The Insurance Factor

Most important, those in the juvenile-justice system say, white youngsters more often have private health insurance, meaning that they may qualify for private treatment and often avoid custody.

"If a kid comes from a home and somebody's working and carrying a Blue Cross card, it's like somebody struck gold," Walavich said. "An insurance card will open up all kinds of doors."

Edward P. Young, who oversees juvenile probation for the San Fernando Valley, agrees.

We find a lot of our white kids who have committed an offense going to in-patient psychiatric facilities before they even get to the court system. An attorney says to the parents, "Get your kids some help and maybe we can get him off."

When they go to court, the court looks at the fact that the kids have spent thirty days in detoxification or treatment, and the judge is likely to just put them on probation or give them credit for that as time served. If it's a serious offense and the court wants detention before the court date, they'll put him in a private psychiatric unit as part of his detention. It's always amazing that the kid is cured just before the insurance runs out.

On one hand, the tactic "is a way for affluent families to avoid having their kid go to detention camp," Young said. "It's a way to manipulate the attitude of the court away from having the kid do hard time." On the other hand, Walavich says, children of affluent families are able to avail themselves of the kind of positive and productive intervention that the public sector should be offering to all.

"Why would a judge or a probation officer or a policeman send a kid to jail before they tried something, if it was possible to try something?" Walavich asked.

And what happens to juveniles who don't have insurance, access to neighborhood counseling facilities, and other diversion resources?

"That black kid is still in juvenile hall waiting for a hearing," Young said. "He's going to sit in detention until his court date comes up. He's probably not going to get any psychiatric counseling. Depending on the situation, he'll go to camp or a suitable placement facility or the California Youth Authority."

"It's not fair or equitable," Judge May says. "It's just the way things are. You've got an impossible situation," he said.

"So you go for the next best alternative, which might not be meaningful. We've got to do something with this kid, and nothing else is available for him. It's not done because it's correct. It's just the only alternative."

It is a disparity played out daily in juvenile courts across the nation. In Los Angeles, a judge sends a thirteen-year-old black boy to youth camp for six months for stealing a radio. He was arrested twice at age twelve for sneaking onto public buses. Though his offenses are minor, a pattern of delinquency appears to be developing. The real problem, apparent to everyone in court, is that he and his sister are being raised by a frail great-grandmother unable to provide adequate direction and control. His parents were lost to him long ago, his mother to drugs, his father to unemployment and despair.

His great-grandmother, though willing, obviously cannot provide what the boy needs, the judge reasons. "Maybe in camp the youngster will learn discipline and control," the judge says. However, at least 43 percent of the juveniles who go through Los Angeles County's youth camps return on new charges, and some studies put the figure much higher.

A black Philadelphia judge voids a fourteen-year-old's probation and places him in custody because he is not attending school regularly. Civil libertarians are outraged. How dare she send a kid to jail simply for not attending school, they fume.

Her response: What hope is there for a black boy in America without an education? At least in custody he must go to classes. Maybe, just maybe, he will get on track.

In Chicago, Judge Walter Williams prepares to sentence a youngster guilty of a relatively minor offense. Williams, the probation officer, and the prosecuting and defense attorneys have all agreed that the youngster should be placed on probation or in some kind of intensive supervision program instead of custody. After hearing from the boy's mother, however, Williams changed his mind and turns the boy over to the state department of corrections for a year.

"His mother begged me to put him in custody," Williams said. "She begged me to take him off the streets. There had been a threat made against his life. She said, 'He will die and he'll be dead if you let him out.' Now, if a mother tells me that and I let that kid go out and something happens to him, I would never be able to live with myself."

The underlying theme, those inside the juvenile-justice system say, is that when parents, police, politicians, public officials, school systems, and community and religious organizations fail to provide a nurturing environment for children, they are dumped on the doorsteps of the nation's judicial system, which has little to offer them but custody.

"It's sad but sometimes that's just it," Williams said. "That's all we have for them."

One State Gives Juveniles a Hand Instead of a Cell

Across the nation, penalties for juvenile offenders are tougher, sentences are longer, facilities are overflowing as the percentage of young Americans behind bars reaches a new high, and the cost of keeping kids in lockup nears $3.2 billion annually.

But, in spite of all this, the number of violent crimes committed by children and youths has begun to rise.

So after seeking increasingly punitive measures for juvenile crime for nearly a generation, many states, cities, and counties are beginning to reevaluate their strategy and to cast about for alternatives.

Dozens of innovative programs are being tested on small scales all across the nation. But justice officials are paying particular attention to Massachusetts, which has a statewide and long-running program that appears to be a success. While spending far less per delinquent than most states, Massachusetts has achieved one of the nation's best records at deterring juvenile crime.

In the 1970s, as most states began to "get tough" on such crime and to pass laws leading to more time in custody, Massachusetts took a different tack.

Today, the state offers what the vast majority of state juvenile justice operations do not. It deals with delinquents on the premise that they require less incarceration, not more; that they belong in smaller facilities, not larger; that they need more supervision, not less.

In Massachusetts only 15 percent of those sent to the state's Department of Youth Services are held in secure, locked facilities. By comparison, nearly all of the juveniles under the supervision of the California Youth Authority are held under lock and key. Only 55 of every 100,000 youngsters in Massachusetts are in custody, contrasted with more than 450 of every 100,000 in California.

Massachusetts has no large, prisonlike facilities housing scores of juveniles. The small proportion of youngsters who are deemed a threat to society are held in fifteen-bed facilities where education, skills, and behavioral development are emphasized, with a teacher-to-student ratio of one to four. The rest—about 1,200 or more than 80 percent of the total committed to the department of Youth Services—are not confined but instead are either given intensive supervision at home or placed in a variety of small, community-based programs, such as group homes.

The result is that in Massachusetts only 23 percent of those committed to the state's youth services programs are incarcerated as repeat offenders, contrasted with 63 percent for the California Youth Authority. And, despite the salaries required for intensive supervision of delinquents, the cost of running the system is nearly half the national average.

"We've cut costs, we've cut repeat offenders, and we don't have a juvenile crime wave," says Ned Laughlin, director of Massachusetts' Department of Youth Services.

The core of the Massachusetts program is the belief that most delinquent children require not custody, but development.

"The public looks for quick and easy solutions," Laughlin says.

> Saying "I'm going to lock up more people," is a quick and easy answer, but it's not the solution. Our nation's incarceration rate is right behind Russia's and South Africa's, and yet we have a higher crime rate than countries who don't have the high lockup rate we have. . . .
>
> What we find is that when we offer a safe, caring environment that holds kids accountable, they respond. Kids are kids. I don't care what they've been doing on the street. They look forward to a reward system. They like a system that is accountable and has positive feedback. It may sound like a small thing, but what a lot of people forget is that these kids are just that—kids.

Many doubted the wisdom of the Massachusetts "experiment," as it was called by those inside the nation's juvenile-justice system, when it was instituted in 1972.

At the time, Massachusetts, like most of the rest of the nation, housed most of its delinquent youngsters in large training schools where more resources were spent on maintaining control than rehabilitating and developing the children.

But Jerry Miller, then director of youth services, argued that the vast majority of youngsters did not require custody. The money spent on keeping them locked up could be better spent solving the personal and behavioral problems that led to delinquency. He abruptly closed all of the state's juvenile detention facilities and moved the youngsters to small, community-based programs or sent them home under supervision.

Believing that more direct guidance and personal attention will get youngsters out of the juvenile-justice system for good at a dramatically lower cost, the state has contracted with a private company to add an extra layer of attention for each child under its KEY Outreach and Tracking Program.

In this program, juveniles whose offenses are often serious enough to mean that they would be placed in custody in another state are kept at home under supervision of youth services officers. In addition, each youngster has a KEY "tracker" with primary responsibility for the child's progress.

The state officer and the tracker meet with the delinquent youngsters and their parents to create a behavioral contract that outlines expectations and goals, as well as stipulates sanctions and rewards based on keeping the contract.

What makes the program work is the extremely small caseload KEY's trackers carry. Each tracker, whose job is to "shadow" the youngsters, has only eight charges. The program costs an average of $9,000 per juvenile annually, instead of the more than $40,000 it costs to keep a child in custody in Massachusetts.

"The tracker is the supervision without walls, because that person is seeing the youngster several times a week, calling the school, taking the kid to the ballgame, visiting and calling the house," Laughlin says. "They're not bound by a nine-to-five schedule. So they act as part big brother and part cop."

Trackers serve not only as monitor of the youngster's movements, but also as broker and advocate for him in his efforts to resume a productive and law-abiding life. If specialized therapies or additional services are needed, KEY workers arrange for them.

The KEY program has been so successful that Missouri, Hawaii, Arizona, and Alabama are attempting to incorporate similar programs into their juvenile justice system.

Though few states have been willing to try to match Massachusetts's massive overhaul of the juvenile-justice system—especially while the public was calling for tougher penalties—a number of states have gradually begun to experiment in smaller ways with alternatives to incarceration.

Derek Diggs, seventeen, is glad Louisiana was one such state. Slightly more than a year ago, Derek was sitting in the Louisiana Technical Institute, the state's equivalent of prison for juveniles, where he had been sentenced to three and a half years after his second arrest and conviction for selling crack cocaine.

Then, in walked Laura Axtel and Lionel Olmstead of the New Orleans Marine Institute, an operation that promises to turn around repeat juvenile offenders *because* it does not put them behind bars. Axtel and Olmstead offered Derek another chance.

Today, Derek, who completed his high school requirements in the program, is enrolled to start school next month at Louisiana's Southern University, majoring in engineering.

New Orleans Marine Institute is one of thirty facilities operated by Associated Marine Institute, a private, nonprofit organization founded twenty-three years ago in Tampa, Florida, with the idea that delinquents can become positive members of society as their self-esteem and respect for others grow. Associated Marine Institute now operates in Arkansas, Delaware, Florida, Georgia, Louisiana, South Carolina, Texas, and Virginia.

Most marine institute programs function like the one in New Orleans in which Derek was enrolled. Juveniles already in custody are selected with a judge's consent and put into the program for up to six months, with the understanding that if they fail, they go back to custody.

Students live at home and travel daily to a site near the city's shipyards. After a daily pep talk and discussion session to iron out student problems, they attend morning classes, where they work to complete a high school equivalency degree. Then they spend the afternoon learning challenging marine activities such as scuba diving or sailing. Participants earn points each day toward promotion to new levels in the program with greater responsibility and more privileges.

"We have a program that's structured for success," says Olmstead, executive director of the New Orleans facility. "We help them set goals and achieve those goals through hands-on work."

Participants spend their nights and weekends at home— where they face the temptations of the streets—for two reasons. First, it cuts costs of the program to $40 a day per youth, contrasted with $120 in lockdown facilities. Second, and more important, institute officials say it teaches youngsters to live successfully in the home and community that first landed them in trouble.

"You're working with the kid within the environment that he's struggling in," says O. B. Stander, executive vice president of operations of the national Associated Marine Institute office in Tampa. "That's where he's going when he gets released. What's there may be bad, but we can't change that right away.

He has to be able to function in that environment without getting in trouble."

After completing the program, youngsters are assigned for three months to "aftercare," a transition program in which a designated worker helps them stay on track.

"What we're trying to do is wean those kids so they are totally responsible for their own success," Stander says. "I don't believe you can drop them off cold turkey and expect them to succeed."

After completing the program, Derek landed a job as a computer clerk. His take-home pay was $282 every two weeks—in contrast to his dope-selling days, when, at fourteen, he sometimes made $700 to $1,000 a day peddling crack cocaine.

Didn't the difference in pay bother him?

"It actually made me feel normal," he says. "When I had as much money as I had and as young as I was, I thought I wasn't even human. You have that on-top feeling. When you've been raised and come up in the lower class all of your life . . . you think you're rich. It's rags to riches in a couple of days. But it all ends. Now I have my mind focused on getting an education and thinking about a future."

The program, Derek says, taught "me that there's more to life than drugs and violence, and that I had what it takes to succeed. I learned that I didn't have to go down the wrong path to get the better things in life."

But most of all, Derek remembers that "if I hadn't gone into the program, right now I'd still be in jail."

Some Juvenile Court officials have made dramatic changes simply by altering their attitude about dealing with juvenile offenders. In Philadelphia, presiding Juvenile Court Judge Frank Reynolds has put his personal stamp on how the city's young offenders are handled.

By dealing swiftly and sternly with hard-core offenders, while offering alternatives to custody and more intense follow-up for new offenders, the city has cut its caseload nearly 10 percent in each of the last three years.

"One thing is certain now about Juvenile Court." Reynolds says. "When a child comes through here, he will be dealt with. When I say he will be dealt with, that doesn't mean we're going to lock him up. It means that we are going to find out exactly what his problems are, what are the issues that led him to commit a crime in the first place. We're not just going to see him and send him away.

"I believe you have to take that approach because, if you ignore children at the outset of their young criminal lives, you're going to have to send them over to adult court when they get to be fifteen or sixteen."

Reynolds's first order of business was to instill a more professional and compassionate attitude among the Juvenile Court judges.

"For a long time Juvenile Court was a dumping ground. There were some good judges, but a lot of them were just serving time before their retirement. We've changed that. You have to have a certain attitude in Juvenile Court. You have to love kids. If you don't love kids, you can't do this job."

Reynolds has sought to expand the list of options that judges have after hearing a case by adding an office whose job is to identify or create the appropriate placement for delinquent youngsters. Now, in addition to custody or probation, judges can choose in-home detention, in which children are confined to home except during school hours; intensive probations, in which they are seen three to four times a month instead of only once; or restitution, which requires them to repay crime victims or perform community service.

Naomi Post gives an example of meaningful restitution:

Community service used to mean kids would go and push a broom or pick up trash, but that wasn't really doing anything in terms of helping turn children away from their activity. It was just time served. We've tried to make that a more meaningful experience, something that deals with the behavior that brought them here.

For example, we had a white kid who was adjudicated on ethnic intimidation for running after a woman and her baby screaming, Nigger, nigger, nigger. We made him do volunteer work at the Martin Luther King Center. We wanted him to see black people in a different light.

It seems to have worked. His attitude changed dramatically. On his own, he went out and found a black Baptist church, started doing cleanup, going to the service.

"In some ways, the court can be the first parent that these kids have had," Reynolds says.

The fact that you live in a house with people who stand in a position of authority over your life doesn't mean you have a parent. A parent is one who nurtures, who advises, who stands as someone to protect you. Most of the kids who come in here are here because they don't have that nurturing, they don't have a person who understands the system well enough to instruct and advise and guide.

The core issue is the family, or the lack thereof. That is the problem that has to be dealt with. The failure or success of a city in dealing with them is reflected in the number of children it has in those maximum security institutions and the intensity with which the children have adopted crime as their vocabulary.

2

Drugs and Teen Violence

Shirley Dicks

An estimated 9 percent of students, ages twelve to nineteen, were crime victims in or around their school over a six-month period. Two percent reported experiencing one or more violent crimes and 7 percent reported at least one property crime. Violent crime in this context largely consists of simple assaults. These crimes involve attacks without weapons and may result in minor injury, such as cuts or bruises. Violent crimes can also include aggravated assaults, robberies, and rapes. Fifteen percent of the students said that their school had gangs, and 16 percent claimed that a student had attacked or threatened a teacher at their school.

Among public school students 9 percent reported it impossible to obtain drugs at school; among private school students, 36 percent reported it impossible to obtain drugs at school. Victimization by violent crime at school had no consistent relation to income levels of the victims' families. In the case of property crime, however, students in families with annual incomes of $50,000 or more were more likely to be victimized than were students whose families earned less than $10,000 per year.

In the first half of 1989 about 30 percent of the students interviewed believed that marijuana was easy to obtain at school. In comparison, 9 percent said crack cocaine was easy to obtain, and 11 percent said powder cocaine was readily available.

Janice

Janice does not have much going for her. She has had a troubled life for all of her fourteen years. Her father is an alcoholic who regularly beats Janice's mother and sexually abused Janice when she was younger. Janice has three older brothers. One of the brothers is severely retarded. The family has no money for his care, so he is simply warehoused at home. The older brothers have moved out after dropping out of school. Janice began skipping school two years ago. Now she is a full year behind her classmates. She also began to shoplift. That was when she first came into contact with the juvenile court. Janice's most recent run-in with the community around her came when she got into a fight at school The parents of the girl she hit pressed charges, and Janice was put on probation for two years. Janice recently became involved with drugs. She ran away from home for over a month. Because she had been taken into custody for her fifth shoplifting offense, she is now in a youth development center.

Arnold

Arnold was one of his thirty-five-year-old mother's seven children. He was exceptionally bright. In elementary school, the teacher found out that Arnold, with other boys, had planned a perfect robbery of the school building. A local minister intervened in juvenile court and took Arnold into his home, only to have the boy run away. Arnold was preoccupied with Easter. On two Easters he set fires in the homes of his grandmother and of neighbors. He ended up in juvenile court, then in the custody of a cousin, and finally in a juvenile home. At fourteen, Arnold seemed to be doing well, but Easter came. He wanted his little brother to have some new clothes, so Arnold robbed a service station. In the confusion that followed the discovery of the theft, Arnold was killed.

Eddy

Eddy is twenty-seven years old; he has been in prison for the last six years. He is currently serving a sentence of fifty-five years for armed robbery. As Eddy looks back at what did or did not happen to him in his life, he reflects, "Young people in trouble sometimes need to talk with someone who has been through it. If you want to know what it is like to be bitten by a dog, you need to ask someone who has been bitten." When pressed for his advice to young people in trouble, Eddy says,

> Know the consequences of your behavior. I always thought that it was some other person who would get caught, not me. Also, find constructive ways to use your time. I had plenty of time on my hands, and I didn't use it well. Now I've got time to do nothing but sit. And pick your friends carefully. I just went along with the crowd, and look where my friends led me. Drugs, that's another piece of advice. Through those same friends I got into drugs, dropped out of school, started doing hard stuff, needed to get money to feed my habit, got a gun, started sticking people up, and here I am. I could have killed somebody.

Finally, sometimes families and youngsters in trouble need outside help; don't be scared of it. I have a volunteer working with me now. I sure wish I'd had him when I was twelve or thirteen.

Eddy is coming up for parole next year. He has a support system waiting for him on the outside. He has the possibility of a job. He has already begun to work with youngsters in trouble. Eddy might just salvage his life, but he will have lost almost a decade of it in the process.

The majority of today's adult criminals were incarcerated as children. Our kids grow up today in a world where drug dealing, mugging, rape, and extortion are a normal part of their lives. Edward M. Davis, former president of the International Associations of Chiefs of Police, issued the following warning: "As the juvenile justice system continues to operate under present constraints, we know that it is building an army of criminals who will prey on our communities. The benign neglect that we have shown has made children with special problems into monsters that will be with us forever. If improvement to the system does not come, it will insure a generation of criminals who will make the current batch look like kids at a Sunday school picnic."

In New York City during the first six months of 1981, there were eighteen homicide arrests of children between the ages of seven and fifteen years. In the same time period, this age group accounted for more than 2,500 arrests for robbery, serious assaults, and rape.

Our human attempts at administering justice have gone seriously awry. The crime problem is not abating, and often the very agency supposed to right wrongs perpetrates injustices. All too often the goal of our criminal justice system is retribution against the wrongdoer; such a goal effects no positive change in either the offender or the offender's situation in the community. Our criminal justice system often reflects the injustices in our society, victimizing the powerless and disenfranchised members of our communities. In accordance with the Presbyterian church, which says that the basic goals of our human agencies of justice need to be carefully evaluated, it is suggested here that the major goal of criminal justice should be reconciliation rather than retribution. Goals of assuring community security, meting out equal justice, bringing restitution to victims, and restoring offenders to the community should replace vengefulness, institutionalized inequalities between races and classes, and the near-permanent alienation of the offender from the community. Our belief in a God who seeks both reconciliation with a sinful humanity and justice for the exploited and oppressed must guide us in the decisions that need to be made.

In any discussion of crime prevention, mention is usually made of tactics such as hiring more police, providing better training for already existing law-enforcement programs, purchasing additional locks and weapons and burglar alarms, marking valuable possessions, increasing prison sentences for convicted felons, and establishing a neighborhood security network run by civilians. Although some of these actions may be necessary in a fallen world, the Gospels call the church to look beyond such strategies to address one of the most basic causes of crime: the lack of community among human beings. The church is herself a group called out to bear witness to God's fellowship with the world in Christ, and to strive toward new fellowship in Jesus' name. So one Christian ethicist with wide exposure to criminal-justice issues can conclude that the most important things we can do to reduce crime are the steps we can take to build and fortify a strong, inclusive community.

In the light of human reason, human decency, and human

dignity, prisons stand as a tragic reflection of the failure of society and ourselves to achieve community. Ironically, prisons victimize not only the keepers and kept alike, but society as well. Lamentably, prisons and jails survive and thrive because of an adherence to the alleged value of punishment that precludes a rational system of individual and community protection.

Prisons and jails are today prime reinforcers of racism in society. They are highly volatile and isolated elements of the criminal justice system. A searching and critical public scrutiny of their internal controls, external policies, and societal influences is lacking. An imperative to replace lethargy with constructive action and misunderstanding with understanding is needed.

For Christians, therefore, an interest in prisoners, prisons, and jails cannot be considered as merely doing something for those "poor unfortunates." Rather, such a concern arises from the uncomfortable awareness that under God there is no difference between those in prisons and those who are not. We give our attention to prisoners not in any objective and disinterested way, but as fellow prisoners with them. We see ourselves in solidarity with those who are prisoners, enjoined to undo a penal system that enslaves us all and that represses the movement of humankind from bondage to freedom.

Many assume prisons exist not only for the just punishment of crimes, but also as an effective deterrent against further commission of crimes. Others assume that prisons exist primarily for the rehabilitation of criminals. The facts clearly show that our penal systems as they presently exist at the federal, state, and local levels are fulfilling the functions of neither deterrence nor rehabilitation. Quite simply, our penal systems are failing.

3

Wrong Side of a Gun

Susan Thomas*

About half the kids taken to Nashville, Tennessee's Metro Juvenile Court each year have been there before. More than 50 percent of juvenile crimes nationwide are committed by 5 percent of the kids. These facts, coupled with multifold increases in violent juvenile crime in Nashville in recent years, are leading to a new emphasis in the battle against youth crime: early intervention. Those who enforce juvenile laws, police and prosecutors, are exploring new ideas. Police here, for example, are discussing a new program that targets kids who have gotten in trouble with the law and are likely to do so again. Under a similar program in Knoxville, Tennessee, the kids are fingerprinted and must carry ID cards. Their behavior is closely monitored and reviewed monthly, to keep small problems from becoming big problems.

Meanwhile, the short-staffed district attorney general's

*Susan Thomas is a staff writer for the Nashville *Tennessean*. Article reprinted with permission.

office will soon begin using law students to prosecute misdemeanor offenses in juvenile court here. The goal is to impress on kids who are not yet in big-time trouble just how serious violating the law can be. Additionally, police and prosecutors are devoting new attention to some nonviolent crimes that have frequently been overlooked in the past. Students caught bringing guns to school, for example, are now often brought to juvenile court on felony charges. In the past, police were seldom even informed when school officials found a gun on a student.

"A lot of people don't understand what we're up against," says Metro Police Homicide Major Pat Griffin. "Most kids just don't get up one day, grab a gun and decide to kill somebody. The problems start a lot earlier. The kids start out shoplifting, committing burglary, or whatever, it's a gradual thing. If we're ever going to do anything about it, it has to be early, before they progress up the ladder to violent crimes."

Local law enforcement officials have felt the tremors of the rapidly rising rate of juvenile violent crime in the past few years. But a blaring wake-up call has come recently through the escalating number of crimes, and from the cries of victims, or from the families of murder victims left behind. A ten-month investigation by the *Tennessean* of violent youth crime between 1970 and 1993 in Davidson County, Tennessee, shows that violent-crime arrests of children younger than eighteen have leapt dramatically, especially in the past five years. In Nashville, in 1989 three juveniles were charged with murder. Last year, that number skyrocketed to twenty-one. In the same five years, juvenile rape arrests rose from 37 to 48, juvenile robbery arrests climbed from 235 to 408, juvenile aggravated assault arrests jumped from 74 to 232. Though most public attention focuses on juvenile murders, Griffin says it is a mistake to minimize the seriousness of other violent crimes. "The only difference between aggravated assault and murder is about an inch, depending on which way the bullet goes," he says.

These trends have accelerated the urgency of law enforcement officials to move more quickly than ever to battle youth crime before it becomes violent. One idea comes from Metro Police Youth Services Capt. Valerie Meece, who wants to identify and monitor potentially dangerous kids earlier. "Basically, it would be sharing information so that we could identify and focus on the kids who need help now, before they became violent offenders," says Meece. As Meece envisions the program, a team of youth services officers would be formed to consolidate information on juveniles now committing minor crimes. That information is available, but scattered in the files of Metro schools, juvenile court, the Davidson County District Attorney General's office, other divisions of Metro Police, as well as support agencies, such as the state department of human services.

Once the information is assembled, Meece says, youth services officers would identify the children most at risk of becoming violent, then develop a plan for each child. The goal would be to intervene with appropriate treatment at the critical time, before the kids become violent.

Rick Autery can't forget the sound—*pow!* "The shotgun blast was extremely loud," says Autery, now twenty-one, recalling the moment on April 14, when his best friend, David Williams, was shot in the stomach. "I looked at David, I was standing right next to him, and I saw a hole before I ever saw any blood. I mean it was that quick, quick enough for me to look and see no blood, but it seemed so slow. David ran backwards and fell on the floor. I ran straight to him and held his head in my hands. Then he started bleeding everywhere. The last thing he said was 'I'm dying.' I told him no, that he wasn't going to die, that he was going to make it."

Hugh David Williams, two months past his nineteenth birthday, died five hours later in surgery at Vanderbilt University Medical Center. He left behind his best friend, his parents, an older sister, a younger brother, and a girlfriend three months pregnant with his child. Today, nothing can take away their pain, especially because the shooting never had to happen. All it was, all it ever should have been, was a simple argument among a group of teenagers. Had it happened a decade or two ago, most likely the fight would have ended with a couple of black eyes or a bloody nose.

But this is the 1990s, and Williams died a 1990s death, killed senselessly, on the wrong side of a gun fired by a juvenile. Daniel Wainscott, then seventeen, pleaded guilty last year to the second-degree murder of Williams. He is serving a fifteen-year prison sentence that most likely will keep him locked up for about five years. "I definitely made the wrong choice," Wainscott says today, explaining how he chose to pick up a shotgun that night instead of running away.

"If the gun hadn't been there, it would have been much better. I mean, I would have probably gotten beat up, but that would have been so much better."

There's no doubt American society, with Nashville in tow, has changed in the past two decades. Many advances have enriched our lives. Other changes, especially those that affect the children of the 1990s, have not. More working women. Absent fathers. Teen-age mothers. Latchkey kids. Domestic violence. The demise of the extended family. Television violence, rap music, poverty, guns, gangs, drugs.

The list goes on, as everyone from politicians, police, and parents to teachers, journalists, and lawyers, searches for reasons to explain the explosion in juvenile crime. The answer is elusive. No one has pinpointed a solution and been able to show that it will work. A ten-month investigation by the *Tennessean* has found that the reasons for the new wave of violence are often tangled and intertwined. There is often no single reason why, no one place to lay all the blame.

A small number of violent juveniles are diagnosed as sociopaths, individuals incapable of feeling compassion or remorse, kids who just don't care. But, experts say, most violent kids today are children who somehow fail to acquire basic living skills such as respect, self-esteem, trust, character traits that could help them stop before they pick up a weapon and rob, rape, assault, or kill.

Still, as Nashville and the nation have scrambled to understand the alarming surge of youth violence, some things offered as causes appear less valid than others.

Guns

Statistics show that there are more weapons on the streets today than ever. Twenty years ago, however, firearms owned by parents and kept in the homes of Nashville children were plentiful. And in Davidson County, Tennessee, juvenile arrests for gun violations, while rising and falling slightly through the years, have only increased from 153 in 1970, to 180 in 1990. One difference, police say, is that twenty years ago, kids were taught not to touch, much less fire, a gun unless supervised by adults, and the kids obeyed.

Drugs

After drug arrests of Nashville youths soared from 48 in 1970 to 369 in 1980, the number actually declined to 358 in 1990.

This takes the wind out of the argument that drugs are the primary reason for today's youth violence, because drug arrests have dropped while violent juvenile crime has soared.

Working Women

National trends of working mothers with children younger than eighteen have continued a slow, steady rise since 1970, when an estimated 42 percent of mothers worked outside the home, compared with 67 percent in 1992. But these increases have come in degrees, in no way resembling the spike of violent youth crime apparent in the late 1980s and early 1990s.

To put a perspective on the many factors that influence juvenile crime, experts say all of the possible causes must be taken into account to understand the overriding fact that American society has changed. Gone are the "Leave It to Beaver" days of Ward and June Cleaver. Instead the nation and the Nashville community is a new society in which, for countless reasons, violent crime thrives and people die.

David Williams is one of more than 120 men, women, and children who have died at the hands of kids in Nashville since 1970. The willingness of Williams and Wainscott's families and friends to share their histories and thoughts, however, offers an unusual insight into the dynamics of why this murder happened.

"I think all adopted kids have some type of something back in their head. . . . Why was I adopted? Why did my parents give me up?" says David's mother, Robbie Williams. Robbie and her husband, Ray, adopted David and his younger brother Joey, now eighteen, when they were young children. "His real dad never bothered calling them, never came to see them. I'm sure that bothered David. When he didn't call them, I'm sure

David and Joey wondered, they really wondered why he didn't."

"David had no fear," Rays says. "He had a heart as big as this house, but he had no fear. I mean, he was a very lovable child, but he was the type of child that once his head was set, you didn't change him. And when he grew older, he's the type of kid that when he was out, if anything happened between a friend and someone else, David would always step in front of it. He had rather get hurt himself than see somebody else get hurt. He was just that way." Ray says his oldest son's fearlessness haunted him.

"I'd always tell him, 'Son, anybody with no fear will get hurt,' " Ray remembers. "I said, 'with no fear, life will be short.' " Those words were prophetic.

"My parents divorced when I was two," says Danny Wainscott's mother, Martha Wainscott, thirty-six, who has three sons younger than Danny, ages fifteen, thirteen, and twelve. "My mama raised me and my four brothers by herself. She worked as a meat cutter at a grocery store to support us, but she was an alcoholic. The social workers in Ohio where we grew up were always trying to take us away from her, but they didn't.

"We stayed together, but since there was never enough money, we ended up moving from place to place, whenever we got evicted."

Martha never married Danny's father, a man Danny has never met. During Danny's early childhood, his mother worked at menial jobs outside the home. When Martha married, other problems arose. Her new husband was so physically abusive, Martha says, that four times she sought treatment for injuries she received at his hands. He left town last year and could not be located for comment. And money was tight. "We couldn't afford to make Danny look the way he wanted to, with clothes and everything," his mother says. "So, just to compensate, he started showing off at school and stuff. He was just always trying to fit into a certain crowd. I call them the 'wannabe' crowd. They just 'wannabe' something more than what they are, they want to be tough, to control the world. Danny wanted people to follow him. He didn't want to follow anyone."

"I met both of them in ninth grade," Amanda Keown says of Danny and David, who were classmates with her at McGavock High School. It was at her apartment on Smith Springs Road that the fatal argument erupted. "We were just all sitting around, talking and watching a movie." Amanda recalls. "I don't even remember what we were talking about but we were just laughing and having a good time."

It was a Tuesday night. It wasn't a party. No alcohol. No drugs. Not even a loud stereo. It just happened that David, out with several of his friends who knew Amanda, stopped by to say hello. A while later, Danny showed up with one of his friends who had asked Amanda if he could move in for a few days until he could find a place. Danny and David had never been friends but they had traveled similar paths. They both dropped out of school in their junior year, got jobs, and tried to make it on their own.

But they both regretted leaving school and when they arrived at Amanda's place, both had decided to better their lives. David wanted to go back to school; Danny wanted to join the Army. As the teens socialized, another boy telephoned the apartment. From that point in the evening the stories become blurred. Danny says a mindless argument erupted among the teens about who were friends and who weren't.

During this argument, David says, he remembered earlier carrying upstairs his friend's belongings, including a shotgun. "I had a choice," Danny says. "Should I run and have them chase me or should I go upstairs and get the shotgun? It was in my mind to frighten them, to keep them away so we could leave."

"Danny was waving the gun around the room at everyone," Rick Autery says. "He was telling us to back off." Amanda, who was upstairs talking with David, remembers hearing strange noises. "David and I went down the stairs at the same time," she says. "Everybody else was already down there. When I saw Danny with the gun, I wasn't scared. I was mad. I yelled something like, 'What the hell are you all doing? What's going on?' And then I started yelling at Danny to get out of my house. He was pointing the gun at all of us at one point or other. When I was screaming, he was pointing the gun at me. I just didn't want any trouble. But then, everyone was yelling."

Within minutes, Danny and his friend agreed to leave and started walking backwards toward the front door. "We were pretty close to them when David tried to wrestle the gun to get it away from him to make him leave," Rick remembers. "Finally, David let go of the gun. Danny had his back to the floor. And then, Danny just kind of pointed the gun at David and shot him. There was no accident to it."

Today, Danny disagrees, as he has done since he turned himself in several days after the shooting. "There's a lot of things I should have done, but I chose a lot of wrong choices," says Danny, insisting that the shooting was accidental.

David's girlfriend, Deidra Kincaid, seventeen, recalls sitting in the hospital waiting room with David's parents. "I just sat there and said like, 'You're supposed to be doctors. You're supposed to be able to do things like this, to save him.' And that's all I remember until they said we could go in there and see him. Ray and Robbie didn't want to go. My mom took me back there. I threw up. It didn't even look like David at all. I just kept talking to him until the nurses took me out."

David Scott Kincaid Williams was born six months after his father's funeral. Today, the two most important people in the baby's life are his mom and his Uncle Joey, his dad's kid brother. Deidra and Joey, even at their young ages, are already afraid of the kind of life David might hope for without a father in a society they now understand has gone astray. "What am I going to tell our son when he's old enough to understand? I don't know. I just don't know how to put it all in words. All I can say now is that I hope and pray our baby grows up in a better world than the one his dad lived in."

It was a chance encounter on a warm afternoon in September 1974. Alarie Lamont Watson, then seventeen, recalls that he was just hanging out, standing on the sidewalk in Nashville when a car pulled up and stopped. "Want a ride?" Those, he says, were the first words that he heard Fisk University ballet instructor Raymond Clay, thirty-two, ever say. "I'd never seen him before, but I said sure, because I wanted a ride out to my mother's house on Clarksville Highway. He seemed nice enough to me, and when he was letting me out, he told me to call him if I ever needed another ride." Watson recalls calling Clay for another ride two nights later. Within hours Clay's nude body was found beneath a pile of bloody blankets in the Fisk dance studio. There was a single bullet wound in his chest. The next morning, Watson turned himself in to police. He pleaded guilty to second-degree murder and was sentenced to twelve years in prison.

Today, Watson is thirty-six. But when he opens the door of his small East Nashville duplex, he looks older, with scars visible on his right side, extending from his ear down to his long, thin fingers. He wears military fatigues, black cowboy boots, and a baseball cap turned backward.

"I've been dealing with what I done, but I haven't forgotten," he says. "The morning after it happened, I felt like what I had done was wrong. Like I was damned, like I was evil, like I was going to hell."

In police interviews that morning, Watson says he was scared and told investigators he first met Clay the night of the murder. "I was just trying to figure out how to get out of this mess," he says. Since that morning in 1974, Watson has spent seven years in prison and mental institutions within the state correctional system, until he was freed June 15, 1981. He says he told correctional officers he did not want to be released—he told them he wanted to do more time, but they told him he'd already done his time. Now, nineteen years have passed since the murder, late that September night.

Clay's family still mourns his death. They choose not to speak about it. Clay's death was a cold-blooded murder. And though Watson says he now knows he did not have to kill Clay, he can look back and understand why he thought he had a reason to kill that night. "I called him and said I needed a ride out to my mother's again. But when he came and picked me up on the same street corner, he said he needed to stop by his studio at Fisk for something. On the ride to North Nashville, he touched me where I didn't want to be touched by a man. I just froze. He didn't say nothing. I didn't say nothing. Then, in about a minute, he put his hand back on the steering wheel."

Watson says that at that point in his life, he knew nothing about homosexuality, only that he remembered, "As a child of five, an older man touched me with his private around my shoulders and then gave me fifty cents." Watson says the second and last time the older man tried to touch him, he cut the man with a razor. But, Watson says, he wasn't thinking of that when Clay invited him into the dance studio, at least not until a few minutes later when he says, Clay touched him again.

"I said, 'Man, what are you doing?' " Watson recalls. "Then he said he wanted me, that he wanted me to call him baby; I just kept saying, 'What are you doing this for, man? What are you doing?' And then I lost my temper. I was getting madder and madder and madder. At that moment, I decided to kill him."

Deliberately, he says, he asked where the rest room was. He walked inside, closed the door, and took out the small pistol he carried, "just to be tough like my friends." Then, Watson said, he carefully wrapped the gun in toilet paper to hide it and walked back into the studio. "The lights were out, but I could see his shadow. He was naked. And he was saying these things, a lot of fantasy sex things that people should keep to themselves. I knew I was going to kill him, but I played around with it. I told him to lay down, and then I laid down on top of him. I had the gun in my hand, pointed right at his heart, and I shot him."

Before running away, Watson says, he covered Clay's body with blankets because "I felt a little sorry for him and didn't want somebody to come in and see him naked." It wasn't until the next morning, he says, that he realized he did not have to kill Clay. "I could have hit him with my fists. It wasn't until I was in prison that the full moral impact of what I had done hit me."

During his years in prison Watson attempted suicide at least twice. Today, he says, he handles what he did as best as he can, but he doesn't forget. "I've never had a conversation with his family," Watson said. "But if I did have, I would tell them I'm sorry, that all I wish is that it never would have happened. Haunted since he killed a man nineteen years ago, Alarie Lamont Watson, now advises teens; "Stop trying to impress your friends, being tough with guns and tough talk, because you don't have to be Clint Eastwood; just be yourself and be a nice person."

You may see them on the street corner. They may go to school with your kids. Or, if you're lucky, you've seen them only on the front page of the newspaper, as they are arrested and taken to juvenile court. They are the new breed of wantonly violent kids whose rage is terrifying Nashville and the nation. "Imagine you felt like this," says Hunter Hurst, director of the National Center for Juvenile Justice in Pittsburgh, which monitors crime nationwide.

"Life has dealt me a raw hand because my daddy was gone before I was born. I was born into filth and trash and hunger, and those around me look the same way. And my mother left me early because she had to work to try and feed us. I see myself as essentially a person of despair, so, then, what else do I have to lose? What does it matter if I off somebody?"

Those are the feelings of many children who become violent young criminals, say Hurst and other national experts studying the wave of violent juvenile crime sweeping America—and Nashville, Tennessee. "We have a lot more young folks and adults in this country who have never resolved their rage about all the things that have happened to them in childhood," Hurst said. "I relate that to the matter of valuing or devaluing life. When life means little or nothing, it's a dangerous signal. That loss of humanity, experts say, creates a boiling cauldron that sets the perfect stage for youngsters to commit random acts of brutal violence against family, friends, or strangers, often for no reason." And Nashville, according to Hurst, may have more than its share of kids who commit violent crimes.

Today, with kids committing more crimes, and the nature of the acts becoming more vicious, experts continue to search not only for the root causes but also for solutions. "Research consistently points out that while it seems as though the rate of juvenile violent crime is increasing, that doesn't necessarily follow and mean that there are more kids committing these crimes," says Deborah Willis, a research associate in the School of Social Work at the University of Michigan. "It's a small group of kids, about 6 to 7 percent of the total juvenile population, who are committing an inordinate amount of these violent offenses." Willis says these children are a very definable group. "They are, for the most part, younger kids who start their criminal activity at age twelve or thirteen, at least below age fourteen. They are kids who commit offenses frequently; this is not something that happens once every couple of years. The offenses stay serious, chronic, and the offenses themselves are of a serious enough nature that we aren't going to feel safe with these kids on the streets."

After all the years of research, Willis says, experts know that unfortunately, there is certainly an overrepresentation of kids in this category who are poor and minorities. "There's been a lot of effort to explain that," she adds, "from people debating the causes of juvenile delinquency and coming up with whether hopelessness leads to a sense of anger, and therefore, they are bad-character people, suggesting these are just bad kids.

"But now, some people are beginning to say, 'Look , it doesn't matter what all the reasons are because violent crime is happening and we've got to do something about them because we're losing a whole generation of kids.' "

After the blast, Alfred Charles Borum, sixteen, swaggered across five lanes of Saturday night traffic on Lafayette Street to rejoin his friends, casually tucking his .32-caliber pistol back inside his jacket. The gun was still hot. "Bro, did you shoot that guy?" screamed his stepsister, watching smoke rise from the revolver into the cold air on February 22, 1992, in South Nashville, Tennessee.

"Yeah," said Borum with a smile. "I shot the m.-f." Minutes before, at about 8:50 P.M., Michael Wayne Swann, Jr., seventeen, a blue-eyed, red-haired senior at Donelson Christian

Academy, had become lost. He had pulled his 1985 red Ford Ranger pickup truck into Eddie's Cee Bee Food Store to ask directions.

Until that moment, Swann, an only child and high school track star, had a life with loving parents and lots of friends. He bagged groceries as his after-school job at a store similar to Eddie's in the suburbs and had dreams of conquering college before meeting the world head on to live a long, happy life. Instead, he met Borum or, at least, Borum's bullet. The single metal slug crashed through the glass of the driver's-side window of his truck, smashing into Swann's left side, carving a path of death that not even the best doctors at Vanderbilt University Medical Center could stop.

So, Michael Swann died that night. Why? "I don't know," Borum says today, shrugging his shoulders. "I was really spaced out at the time." Swann's mother remembers the night differently, and vividly. "The night Mike was murdered, I just went through the whole house screaming for him," says Debbie Swann Fultz, shivering at the memory. "Then, I don't know, I went numb. I guess I went into sort of shock. And even now, today, if I could only understand why it happened, why he shot him, why my child, why Mike had to die. . . ." Her voice trails off into tears.

"I'm sorry. I said I wasn't going to cry. But just when you think you've shed all the tears you can just wondering why, you can't get it out of your mind." The official facts found in police file #92-48795 are starkly simple. When Swann stopped to ask directions, Borum decided to rob him. When Swann wouldn't open his truck door, Borum tried to, causing the truck's burglar alarm to sound. Then Borum took a step back, leveled his gun barrel, and fired. Swann died.

Borum pleaded guilty to second-degree murder and was

sentenced to twenty-five years. He will most likely be free after eight or nine. "Those are the facts," says Metro Homicide Maj. Pat Griffin, "but they don't explain why this guy shot that young boy for absolutely no reason at all. It's just senseless. Crazy."

Two months before Swann's murder, Borum was sent to Metro Juvenile Court for assaulting a teacher at Whites Creek High School. "I was just sitting in the bleachers, and this teacher dude came up and grabbed a bag of potato chips out of my hand," Borum says, "so I jumped up off the bleachers and started hitting him with my fists." Borum was expelled from school on the resulting assault charge. He was sentenced to perform community service work. Borum says he cannot remember how many hours juvenile court gave him.

A week later, after performing nine hours of public service, he moved in with a girlfriend living at the J. C. Napier housing development on Lafayette Street.

Once there, Borum says, he forgot about serving the public service work at a local community center because they wouldn't fit the hours into his schedule. So, out of school for weeks, Borum says, he spent his days baby-sitting in the housing project and his nights drugging and drinking.

"I wasn't in school. I felt like this, this pressure plying down on me. I was in a no-win situation. I wasn't getting anywhere." Borum was in a situation, he says, not unlike the one his father had once been in. "My father went to prison for murder when I was about four," Borum says. "My mother used to take me to visit him. I remember he used to tell me, 'Don't do this and don't do that,' about getting into trouble and all, but I thought, 'How can he tell me? He's locked up inside?' "

Today, that sense of defiance still seems a part of Borum's life. When he was asked what he would say to Swann's parents if he had the chance, he said, "I would say I'm sorry, but that ain't going to bring back their son's life. I just made a mistake in life."

And after saying he believes in God, when asked if he thinks he will go to heaven or hell, he says, "I really can't say at this time." Instead, Borum, a muscular eighteen-year-old who wears his hair in corn rows and a tiny earring in his left ear, vows from his West Tennessee prison cell to be a model inmate. He says he wants to do the quickest prison time possible.

Two hundred miles away each Saturday, Swann's mother walks through Goodlettsville's Forest Lawn Cemetery to her son's grave. She decorates it for the changing seasons and special holidays.

She's getting ready for his birthday, March 23. He would be twenty. "Sometimes it's almost like I put it out of my mind," she says softly. "I'll pretend Mikie's away at college or something, and he'll be back. But I know it's not real. He'll never be back."

4

The Mentally Retarded and the Justice System

Robert Perske* and Shirley Dicks

Johnny Shouldn't Be in Jail

For his first twenty years, Johnny Lee Wilson lived a warm, well-protected life in Aurora—until a fateful day in 1986. Before that day, almost everyone in this southwestern Missouri town of 6,340 knew this shy, unathletic young man with the contagious smile. They knew how his mother, Susan, and his grandmother, Nellie Maples, took his mental disabilities in stride and shared in his parenting.

The Aurora public schools adjusted to Johnny's "organic brain damage and mental retardation," provided him with special education classes, and helped him follow his own rate of development for twelve full years. His teachers described him as "quiet, reserved, respectful," and "never a discipline prob-

*Robert Perske is the author of *Unequal Justice?* and *Circle of Friends*. The first part of this article, "Johnny Shouldn't be in Jail," by Robert Perske, originally appeared in the *Kansas City Star,* February 20, 1994. Reprinted by permission.

lem." After graduation, Wilson had sporadic lawn-mowing jobs to which his mother drove him.

Even investigators of the murder of seventy-nine-year-old Pauline Martz found Wilson likable. Sergeant J. J. Bickers said of him, "He was a nice kid. He was polite—yes, sir; no, sir. He was easy to talk to. The only problem is, he killed her."

Wilson will soon begin his seventh year in the penitentiary at Jefferson City. He is doing life without parole because law officials believe that for one day—just one day in his life—he became an overpowering savage. They believe he methodically ripped up every room in the Martz home, looking for valuables to steal. They believe he tied up Mrs. Martz and set the house on fire.

Interestingly, no physical evidence has ever connected Wilson to the murder. The whole case is based on a confession the police bullied him into making. Some prosecutors, however, feel the confession is the *queen* of the case; with that nothing else is needed.

As a writer and consultant in mental retardation who has followed over a hundred vulnerable people who have "confessed" to crimes they did not commit, I believe Wilson is innocent. Here is the sequence of events that lead me to this belief.

Sunday, April 13, 1986. Wilson, his mother, and his grandmother attended morning services at First Presbyterian Church. At noon, a friend came over and stayed until Wilson was driven by his mother to a lawn-mowing job. Afterward, Wilson, his friend, and the grandmother watched a Disney TV program. After the show, the boys taped songs until suppertime. Upon finishing supper, Wilson and his mother drove to the post office and Ramsey's Supermarket. Leaving Ramsey's they heard sirens and followed the fire trucks to the home of Pauline Martz.

Monday, April 14. Joplin Police Lt. Dick Schurman called local officers and told them about Chris Brownfield, a Joplin native who had escaped from an Oklahoma prison. Schurman said that Brownfield "has been known to tie up and beat old ladies and is more than capable of murder."

Tuesday, April 15. Officers questioned Wilson in his home. Earlier, they had received a tip from one of his former special education classmates who claimed that Wilson had said he killed Martz. The boys' former teacher described the informer as one who often told lies to get attention.

Friday, April 18. Wilson was taken to the police station and interrogated from 9:30 P.M. until after midnight. The police were rough ("Murder is what you're in on. Murder! Premeditated, willful, malicious, burning up an old lady in her house! That's what you're in on, Wilson. Ain't no sense kidding around about it.") Wilson denied it ("I wasn't near that house, though"), but the officer continued his pressure ("I think it's despicable!"). Around 1:00, the next morning, Wilson signed a confession.

After Wilson finally began to break down, one listening to the audio tapes can hear a ludicrous set of interchanges as an officer led Wilson into giving the color of the victim's blouse. Wilson tried to say what was used to bind the victim's ankles. "I'm thinking. . . . Handcuffs, I think." "No. No. Wrong guess," the officer replied. Mrs. Martz's ankles had been bound with duct tape.

On the May 12, 1990, broadcast of CBS/TV's "Saturday Night with Connie Chung," Wilson told Chung he became frightened when the officers "grabbed my face and turned it toward them." Later, "a cop said, 'Well, if you confess . . . we can all go home.' At that point I thought he meant me too."

April 15, 1987. A competency hearing was held before Jasper County Circuit Judge L. Thomas Elliston in Joplin. Psychologist Daniel Foster and psychiatrist William Logan, representing the defense, testified that Wilson was not competent to stand trial because of brain damage, mental retardation, and a dependent personality disorder. Fulton State Hospital psychiatrist Mahinda Jayaratna stated in a written report for the prosecution that Wilson was competent. Judge Elliston ruled in favor of the prosecution.

April 30, 1987. In a plea hearing, Judge Elliston repeatedly reminded Wilson that if he went on trial, he could get death. In one of many interchanges, the judge asked, "Do you want the death penalty?" "No," said Wilson. "Do you want to avoid the death penalty?" "Yes." "Are you admitting that you committed this murder?" "Yes," Wilson said, even though he told the judge at one point that he didn't know exactly why he was pleading guilty.

February 1988. Chris Brownfield confessed to murdering Martz. He made the confession from inside the Kansas State Penitentiary where he is now serving a life sentence for murdering an elderly woman in Pittsburgh, Kansas, sixty miles northwest of Aurora, just sixteen days after Martz was killed. He also described a stun gun he lost in the Martz home—which the police found but never made public. The fire had been set to destroy fingerprints on the gun.

September 12, 1990. In Springfield, public defender William J. Swift gave the Missouri Court of Appeals seven reasons for vacating Wilson's guilty plea: his impaired development; his activities on the day of the crime; a faulty police investigation; the competency hearing and Judge Elliston's conduct; Brownfield's admission of responsibility; Wilson's responses at the plea hearing; and his inability to consult with plea attorneys in a meaningful fashion.

Assistant Attorney General Elizabeth Ziegler argued that it was too late for new evidence to be introduced. The court should only decide whether the legal procedures had been conducted in accordance with the laws of the state—no more and no less. Two months after the hearing, the court sided with Ziegler.

November 11, 1990. The Martz case was aired on NBC's "Unsolved Mysteries." Auroran Lucille Childress, age seventy-four, watched the program, then she contacted the *Marionville New Press.* She said she had seen Wilson and his mother at Ramsey's on the night of the crime. "I came out right behind them," she said. Then when the sirens sounded, she overheard the mother and son deciding to "go see where the fire is." Her earlier silence stemmed from a fear that her relatives would be harmed.

May 9, 1991. Public defender Swift brought the case before the Missouri Supreme Court in Jefferson City. This time, however, his efforts were supported by a "friend of the court" brief submitted by the American Association on Mental Retardation (AAMR) and signed by four attorneys.

One hour before the hearing, Swift submitted to the justices a transcript of an audio tape conversation between Brownfield and his alleged accomplice in the Martz killing. It had been delivered to the AAMR attorneys and Swift by former Kansas Attorney General Vern Miller. Miller, now in private practice in Wichita, arranged for Brownfield to make the telephone contact. The tape convinced Miller that Brownfield and the accomplice had murdered Martz and that Wilson was innocent.

In the recorded conversation, the alleged accomplice confronted Brownfield immediately for: "talking too much for my likes, brother." Brownfield said he couldn't "leave the kid laying in there like that," and he described how officials needed the accomplice's name before releasing Wilson. "After about an hour I finally said, well, ——— was with me." To that, the accomplice responded. "Well, thanks, God damn. It took you a whole hour to cop me out."

This surprise submission stimulated questions from the justices about whether they could indeed consider this new evidence or whether it could only be placed in the hands of the governor. Ziegler again argued that it was too late for new evidence to be admitted. Later the court agreed with Ziegler.

Wilson lives in prison because of a confession he made with no physical evidence to back it up. Doug Seneker, one of Wilson's interrogators, said in the September 8, 1990, *Springfield News Leader* that the confession is just.

"There is a principle in interrogation," he said. "A person will not admit to something they haven't done, short of torture or extreme duress. No matter how long you're grilled," he continued, "no matter how much you're yelled at, you're not going to admit to something you haven't done."

I disagree. The courts of the land are beginning to see that many vulnerable people with dependent personalities survive in the community by trusting good authority figures and by looking to them for guidance.

Wilson tended to function that way and it amounted to a good life for him—until he was brought into a police interrogation room. Then this propensity was used against him. They pressured him. They shaped his words. They solved the case.

The only problem: They convicted the wrong man.

Only the governor can get him out of prison now. If it doesn't happen soon, Johnny could disappear in prison. Write if you would to Governor Mel Carnahan, 216 State Capital, P.O. Box 720, Jefferson City, MO 65102.

Characteristics of the Mentally Handicapped That Can Lead to Victimization

When persons with retardation or other developmental disabilities get arrested, the outcomes are usually fair and just. Once in a while, however, they confess to crimes they did not commit. Local law officials and individuals who work with persons with disabilities may profit from meeting together and discussing the characteristics of mentally retarded people that can lead them to make false confessions.

1. *Relying on Authority Figures for Solutions to Everyday Problems.* For most people, life's zest comes from solving their own everyday problems. Some of us, however, may not be so good at figuring out what to say and do in certain situations. So we try to get close to authority figures who seem to have the answers. That's why many persons with retardation respect police officers and seek them out as friends.

2. *The Desire to Please Persons in Authority.* This urge stems from both respect and fear. One needs to stay on the good side of those who help us survive in the community. In many confessions one can sense this desire in statements like, "If the detective said I did it, then I guess I did, even though I can't remember doing it."

3. *The Inability to Abstract from Concrete Thought.* When someone reads the Miranda Rights to certain persons with retardation, they may only grasp these rights in concrete terms. They may think of things like "waving at the right"—after all, nobody should wave at the wrong in a police station. They may think about their right hands and consider raising them. They may be unable to grasp the abstract thought that Miranda Rights are based on a person's Constitutional rights as a citizen.

4. *Watching for Clues from the Interrogator.* Some persons look closely at another's face and listen for emphases placed on certain words, trying to sense what an officer wants to hear. The person may even copy moods in order to come up with answers the officer wants.

5. *The Longing for Friends.* Some persons hunger for friends who won't shy away from them because of their dis-

abilities. Many would love to have a police officer as a good friend.

6. *Relating Best with Children or Older Persons.* When people their own age don't take to them, they often work at befriending those who are younger or older.

7. *The Plea Bargaining of Accomplices.* Often this hunger for friends can get a person hooked up with the wrong friends. Then, when both are apprehended for a crime, the so-called normal suspect plea bargains for a lesser sentence by testifying against the person with the disability, who then gets the book thrown at him or her.

8. *Bluffing Greater Competence than One Possesses.* Persons with disabilities sometimes do everything they can to appear more knowledgeable then they really are. An untrained officer can easily reinforce this cloak of competency and use it against them.

9. *An All-Too-Pleasant Facade.* Smiling at people is a way of getting approval from others. An officer might see this overuse of grinning as a lack of remorse.

10. *Abhorrence for the Term "Mental Retardation."* This term has wounded some persons so deeply, they'll do almost anything to disconnect themselves from it. If a prosecutor is trying to argue that a person is not retarded, that defendant might seal his own doom by agreeing with him.

11. *Real Memory Gaps.* Some people with disabilities have real ones, not the selective memories crafty people exhibit on the witness stand. Some will hide these lapses of memory by claiming to remember what others told them about the crime.

12. *A Quickness to Take the Blame.* Even if the tragedy is an act of God or an unforeseeable accident, some persons will feel that someone must be held responsible. They may even take the blame, thinking the officer will like them more if they do.

13. *Impaired Judgment.* Unlike a crafty criminal with anti-social tendencies, some persons will do and say things that will make it easy for officers to pin crimes on them.

14. *An Inability to Understand Court Proceedings, to Assist in One's Own Defense, and to Understand the Punishment.* In spite of their cloak of competence, some may be completely unaware of what is going on around them.

15. *Problems with Receptive and Expressive Language.* Although they may not show it, some persons will not understand what the officer is asking them. If the officer pushes them too hard, their response system may shut down. The officer may see this silence as sassy defiance.

16. *Short Attention Spans.* Although myriad sights and sounds will strike an officer's sensing mechanisms, he will be able to concentrate on a few and tune out the rest. Some persons with disabilities may not be able to focus as well. They may be distracted by many more sights and sounds in the police station, even a noisy fan, or the sound of voices in another room.

17. *Uncontrolled Impulses.* The officer may feel many impulses, but he or she will act on a few healthy ones and keep the others in check. Persons with certain disabilities may not be able to control their impulses like that. They may be prey to many urges they are feeling. One might be the urge to confess to a crime to reduce the pressure of the situation.

18. *An Unsteady Gait and Struggling Speech.* Persons with cerebral palsy may be excellent receivers of sights and sounds and ideas. But when they try to respond, the impulses sent to their muscles will appear to have been dispatched by a madman. Arms may flail. Heads may bob. The persons will exert tremendous energy trying to shape the words they want to voice.

19. *Seeing Persons with Disabilities as Less than Human.* This view can lead to all kinds of prosecutorial mischief. After

all, just suppose you as an officer were under pressure to resolve a two-year-old crime, and you had, say, two suspects, a local bank president and a person with mental disabilities. Which would be the easiest to lean on? Seeing a person as dumb, as a nobody, as a fringe person or less than human can inspire a cruel advantage that has no place in an interrogation room or a court.

20. *Exhaustion and the Surrender of All Defenses.* If interrogating officers keep persons with certain disabilities under pressure for long periods of time, they can break them down and get them to say almost anything.

Leon Brown, Death Row's Youngest

After being sentenced to death in 1984 Leon Brown, sixteen, of Red Springs, North Carolina, made the news. He was the youngest inmate on death row in the nation. Something else, however, was played down: psychological reports stating that he had an IQ of fifty-eight. Court-appointed trial attorney Robert Jacobsen said he hadn't wanted to overemphasize his client's retardation for fear the jurors would judge him even more harshly.

Jacobsen told reporter Dee Reid, "The problem is when you start thinking about these types of crimes, that's the type of people who commit them." Arguing against Jacobsen in Brown's trial was nationally known prosecutor Joe Freeman Britt, listed in the *Guinness Book of World Records* for securing more death sentences than anyone else on the planet. Britt told the jury that mental retardation was no excuse. "Are you to mitigate or excuse or do away with the actions of Leon Brown because he's just like two-thirds of a million people?" The jury found that neither the defendant's age nor his retardation were mitigating factors. It determined that Brown, along with his older half brother Henry Lee McCollum, nineteen, had brutally raped and murdered a young girl. According to the investigators, McCollum, with an IQ of seventy-four, confessed and implicated Brown. Upon receiving both confessions—the only evidence against the brothers—the investigators ceased to follow up on other hot leads. One Red Springs police officer now declares his firm belief that both Brown and McCollum are innocent. New defense lawyers are seeking retrials.

The Dual-Diagnoses Dilemma of Morris Mason

The state of Virginia electrocuted thirty-two-year-old Morris Mason on June 25, 1985, in spite of his dual diagnoses of mental retardation and mental illness. Mason grew up on the sparsely populated Eastern Shore. Folks knew him as a school dropout, a loner, and the butt of other kids pranks.

He spent time in three mental hospitals, where he was diagnosed as having an IQ of sixty-six and schizophrenic reactions. At age twenty-two he lost control, committed an act of arson, and went to prison. Two-and-a-half years later, he left the prison, but he couldn't adjust to the outside world. Feeling himself rapidly losing control, he called his parole officer twice, asking for help. On May 12, 1978, he called again, asking that he be placed in a halfway house or some kind of supervised environment. The parole officer set a meeting for later that week.

That appointment was never kept because the next day Mason went on an alcoholic rampage, killing a seventy-two-year-old woman and burning down her house. On May 14, he attacked two girls, ages twelve and thirteen, leaving one with paraplegia. He pleaded guilty and waived his right to a trial. Sentenced to death, he left the courtroom talking crazily about being the killer for the Eastern Shore and making the Eastern Shore popular. The Eastern Shore's demand for revenge, understandably, never ceased. On the other hand, judges never stopped the legal machinery long enough to determine whether it was proper to electrocute a person so retarded and mentally ill. Virginia law requires the transfer of any prisoner diagnosed as insane to a mental health facility. The prison warden, however, is solely responsible for initiating a sanity hearing in the case of a condemned prisoner. The man's mental retardation was ignored. Joseph Ingle described Mason on the last day of his life:

> On June 25, 1985, Marie Deans and I visited Morris Mason in the basement of the Virginia State Penitentiary. Morris was scheduled for electrocution at 11:00. Our afternoon visit was spent talking with Morris while he packed his meager possessions in a box. He showed us letters he'd received, proud to have been sent mail even though some letters urged his killing. All Morris understood was that people were writing to him. . . .
>
> At one point, Morris looked up and asked; "What does it mean to die?"
>
> Marie responded: "It means you'll be with your grandmother." That seemed to satisfy Morris, and he chatted on about basketball. Suddenly he stopped and told Marie: "You tell Roger, another death row prisoner, when I get back, I'm gonna show him I can play basketball as good as he can." The concept of death eluded Morris as it does any child. At about 8:30 the death squad came to shave him for electrocution. We had to leave. When we returned we found Morris lying on his bunk, the back of his shaved head glistening

from the light outside the cell. He turned to us and sighed; "Oh Marie, look what they've done to me now."

We sat outside the cell, the minutes slipping away. Marie held Morris's hand. He asked us about death again. Before we could answer, his expression brightened, and he said, "Does it mean I get to order anything I want for breakfast?" For Morris, selecting his own meal after years of being fed in his cell represented the ultimate idea of heaven. As Morris was struggling to articulate thoughts about death and dying, a shout and commotion came from the hallway. . . . I turned around to confront the warden of Mecklenburg Correctional Center, the location of Death Row over one hundred miles from Richmond and the electric chair. He was striding across the basement floor, yelling that he had to have a private conversation with Morris Mason. Marie and I stepped aside. . . . The warden stayed about ninety seconds, asking Morris if he had a message for the men on death row. Morris mumbled a few nothings and the warden left. . . .

At 10:30 and only fifteen more minutes with Morris...the overwhelming feelings of bidding goodbye to a child struck me. As the death squad took Morris away, Marie and I exited through the basement door, walked up into the yard and through the administration building. Outside, the warden was holding court with the press, informing them of how competent Morris Mason was. Suddenly I understood why this warden had made his perfunctory visit to Morris. . . . He spoke for quite some time to the press about his ninety-second conversation with Morris.

After Mason's execution, Joseph Giarratano, a fellow inmate on death row, wrote a touching memoir:

When they executed Morris they didn't kill a consciously responsible individual; they executed a child in a man's body.

To this day, I do not believe that Morris knew right from wrong, or left from right for that matter. He just didn't want anyone to be angry with him. That includes the guards who worked the unit. The guards were always his best listeners; they had to be there for eight hours a shift anyway. And Morris would stand there and babble for as long as they would sit and listen. Back then conditions on the Row were pretty harsh, but nothing seemed to phase him. No one here, prisoner or guard, saw Morris as a threat. If he were here today, he would still be chattering on about sports and trying to please people in his own out-of-touch-with-reality way.

5

Coretta Scott King on the Execution of Westley Allan Dodd

The execution of Westley Allan Dodd, the nation's first legal hanging in twenty-eight years, no doubt brought a sigh of relief to death-penalty supporters as well as his victims' survivors. But when the state murders its own citizens, there is a price to be paid, no matter how vicious the condemned man may be.

In the Dodd case, there was no possibility that he was innocent because he confessed to the most brutal of crimes. But all the death rows of America have inmates who insist that they were wrongfully convicted, and history suggests that some are telling the truth. It happens.

At least twenty-five Americans who were later found innocent have been executed in this century. On average, an innocent person is convicted of murder in the United States once every year, according to the American Civil Liberties Union. Since 1972, at least thirty individuals have been sentenced to death and later found to be innocent, including James Richardson, the Florida migrant worker who was freed in 1989.

There is no getting around the evidence that the lives of

innocent people are threatened by capital punishment. The death penalty makes any possible miscarriage of justice irrevocable. Dodd's unquestioned guilt notwithstanding, his hanging makes it a little easier for wrongfully convicted inmates to be executed.

State-sponsored executions set a dehumanizing example of brutality that only encourages violence. Allowing the state to kill its own citizens diminishes our humanity and sets a dangerous precedent that is unworthy of a civilized society. Of all the industrialized nations, only the United States and South Africa subject their citizens to capital punishment. Having lost a husband and mother-in-law to gunmen, I well understand the hurt and anger felt by the loved ones of those who have been murdered. Yet, I can't accept the judgment that their killers deserve to be executed. To do so merely perpetuates the tragic, unending cycle of violence that destroys our hopes for a decent society.

The death penalty provides short-range satisfaction to the very human impulse to seek revenge. In the long run, however, compounding acts of brutality adds to the suffering of the loved ones of offenders, and sometimes even victims. Revenge and retribution can never produce genuine healing. They can only deprive survivors of the opportunity for forgiveness and reconciliation that is needed for the healing process.

At present, at least thirty-eight states permit the death penalty—ten even allow the execution of pregnant women. More than 1,900 prisoners are currently under the death sentences in these states. Death-penalty supporters argue that the punishment has a deterrent effect. But states that have reinstated the death penalty after abolishing it have not experienced a decline in criminal homicides. A study by the Michigan Prison and Jail Overcrowding Project in 1985 found that Illinois, a death-penalty state, had a higher murder rate than Michigan, a state that has banned capital punishment, for each of the ten years compared.

Although the prevailing belief seems to be that the death penalty saves the taxpayer the cost of supporting a prisoner for life, there is some evidence that executions are even more expensive. A 1982 study found that the average cost of a capital offense trial in New York through the first stage of appeals alone cost about $1.8 million, more than twice the expense of life imprisonment.

The hanging of Westley Allan Dodd gives law enforcement one less killer to worry about. But it has made our state and local governments a little less humane.

6

The Electric Chair

Frank Bambridge

I've been in prison ministry now for about seventeen years and for the past fifteen years I've worked with death-row inmates. To the kids out there I would say that the electric chair is nothing you want to happen to you. This is the final end to a person in Tennessee who has been sentenced to die.

There hasn't been anybody executed in this state for the past thirty-three years and the last man was executed in 1960. And before that, the first man was executed in 1916. In that forty-four-year interval, there has been a total of 145 men executed in the state of Tennessee for serious convictions of murder or rape. The oldest man was fifty-five years old, the youngest, fifteen years old—perhaps the age of some of you kids out there. Like you, he probably didn't think he'd end up in trouble. But he did. And now we've got approximately 101 people on death row in this state. None of them ever thought they'd end up on death row.

I know quite a few death-row inmates personally. I've prayed with them, talked with them, laughed with them, and a few of them have cried with me. A lot of them I care about. A lot of them have parents, girlfriends, wives, children, grand-children. They're human beings, human beings who made mis-takes, led the wrong lifestyle, and eventually it got them where the next stop is this electric chair.

One young man, Ron Harries, came within a day of being executed. He went on death watch and each night I would go spend time with him. It was one of the worst experiences I have ever seen, the electric chair on the other side of the wall to provide instant death if he was put there.

He got a stay, yet he still sits on death row. He's only dodged it, he hasn't missed it. This chair that has often been referred to as "Old Sparky" can put about twenty-five hundred volts through a person when the executioner turns the switch. It's a violent end to a violent life. It is the violent end that a man receives because of a violent act. And it grieves me to think that some of the men and women I care about may someday end up losing their lives by sitting in this chair.

And maybe they, like you, thought they would never end up in a place like this, but they did. And maybe they, like you, thought they could float along in life because the trouble they got into was not something they looked for, was not something they asked for. It was a turning away of responsibilities, it was a turning away from the fact that you are accountable for your actions even though you are only a kid.

I would say to you as you see the electric chair: Take a look at your lives, youngsters. You are accountable for what you do. You're accountable for life. You do not get a free ride. You are responsible for what you do and you can't blame it on your environment. You can't blame it on anything except yourself. You can live a meaningful life by giving to others, so that you or someone that you love and care for does not end up in this chair.

This chair represents the finality of a life that brought pain to the one who will sit in it, and brings pain to the ones you hurt to get yourself here. The time is right now for you to make a right choice. This is not to frighten you; this is to show you the reality of life if you are not accountable for what you do to yourself or to others. This is what can happen to you. I pray that you kids will take your responsibilities in life seriously and will know deep inside yourself that you are the one who makes decisions for your life. You must be responsible for yourself, for I pray that I will never see any of you on death row with the chair.

7

Life without Parole:
An Alternative to the
Death Penalty

Richard Dieter*

A new national opinion survey reveals for the first time that Americans may be ready for a change regarding the death penalty. More people would choose life without parole plus restitution to the victim's family over the death penalty for first-degree murder. But Americans, including many serving on death penalty juries, are unaware that such lengthy sentences are now being regularly applied by most states.

The myth persists that even the most dangerous murderers will be released in seven years if they are not executed. Such misperceptions fuel support for the death penalty and politicians' demands for more executions. Jurors serving in capital cases are equally in the dark, frequently assuming that their choice is between a meaningless life sentence and death. Judges are often forbidden by law from explaining to the jury that inmates must now serve twenty-five, thirty-five, or more years

*Richard Dieter is executive director of The Death Penalty Information Center, 1606 20th Street, N.W., 2nd Floor, Washington, D.C. 20009.

before even becoming eligible for parole. Both in the courts and on the streets, the death penalty rides a wave of misinformation with no basis in current sentencing law.

Contrary to the conventional wisdom that Americans wholeheartedly support the death penalty, the latest national opinion poll released in conjunction with this report shows that more people in this country would prefer alternative sentences that guarantee both protection and punishment over the death penalty. Support for the death penalty becomes a minority opinion when the public is presented with a variety of alternative sentences. Most Americans, however, are unaware that the length of imprisonment embodied in these alternatives is now the norm almost everywhere in the country.

Since its reinstatement in 1876, the death penalty has brought little but frustration to both proponents and opponents alike. The evidence of racism, of innocent defendants, of costs and delay continues to plague this country's recent experiments with the punishment of death. The failure of executions to achieve more than a spectacle has raised the question: Could America live without the death penalty? Are there alternatives to deal with the type of criminals who are currently sentenced to death?

One of society's best-kept secrets is that the lengthy sentences that people would support over the death penalty are already in place and functioning in most of the United States. Forty-five states plus the District of Columbia presently employ a life sentence in which there is no possibility of parole for at least twenty-five years. Thirty-three of those jurisdictions use a life sentence in which parole is never possible. Yet parole information is often withheld from jurors in capital cases, and the use of these severe sentences is unknown to most of the public. As one recent study concerning the public's knowledge about the death penalty concluded, a majority of Americans have taken a very strong position on an issue about which they are substantially uninformed.

In many states the stringent restrictions on release of those convicted of murder are a new phenomena. But in those places where they have been the law for some time, they are working as promised. In California, for example, no prisoner sentenced to life without parole has been released in twenty-five years.

From all indications, America could be safer without the death penalty and would realize an enormous monetary saving as well. Judging by the crime rates in those states that have abolished capital punishment and instituted alternative sentences, the absence of the death penalty would cause no rise in the murder rate. Capital murderers would not be released after serving only seven years. Hundreds of millions of dollars and thousands of hours of court time would be saved by replacing the death penalty with alternative sentences. The money saved could be devoted to crime prevention measures that really do reduce crime and violence and thus are the true alternatives to the death penalty.

People are frightened by press accounts of parole considerations for such notorious criminals as Charles Manson and Sirhan Sirhan. No doubt, people believed that if these criminals are eligible for parole, anyone would be. But neither of these men was sentenced under a life-without-parole scheme, because that penalty had not been enacted when they had committed their crimes. The fact that these and similar cases receive consideration for parole, even though denied, tends to obscure the fact that today such offenders would not even be eligible for parole. In every state, the myth that if people are not given the death penalty they will be released in seven years is simply not true.

People are also disturbed by reports of prisoners who actually are released after a relatively short time, some of whom commit additional crimes. In Texas, for example, there is much confusion about sentencing. Prisoners on the whole are only serving 20 percent of their sentences and recidivism is a serious problem. Typically, even those with a life sentence have been getting out in less than six years, partly due to the overcrowding in Texas prisons.

What is not widely known, however, is that for those convicted of capital murder, the reality is now quite different; a life sentence for them means they will not even be eligible for parole for thirty-five years. However, Texas law forbids either side from informing the jury about the true meaning of a life sentence in a capital case, and so death sentences are being returned under a gross misperception. Jurors, and the public in general, mistakenly believe they must choose between releasing a violent murderer in six years or imposing the death penalty, even though the reality is quite different.

States that have used the sentence of life without parole say it works as promised. California has had a sentence of life without parole for over twenty-five years and not one person sentenced under this law has been released from prison. In Alabama, U.S. Court of Appeals Judge Edward Carnes, who headed the state's capital punishment division as assistant attorney general for many years, said that life without parole in Alabama means just that. No parole, no commutation, no way out until the day you die, period.

When considering the range of alternatives to the death penalty, the length of incarceration is not the only issue to be weighed. The discussion should also include alternatives that help reduce the risk of violence and murder. Crime prevention through community policing and gun control, employment opportunities, drug and alcohol rehabilitation programs, early intervention for abused and mentally handicapped children are all alternatives to capital punishment in that they lower the risk of crime in the first place.

Governments, of course, cannot fund every program that presents itself. Each program, including the death penalty, has its costs. If the death penalty were eliminated, there would be an immediate savings of millions of dollars for countries and states that could be transferred to other programs with proven records for reducing crime. In the final analysis, it is these alternatives that actually address the rise in violence that prompted this country's return to the death penalty.

It is sometimes argued that the death penalty is necessary to assuage the grief suffered by the family of the murdered victim. For some families that may be true. However, in a country with twenty-five thousand murders and twenty-five executions per year, only one in a thousand families will actually receive such a benefit. The rest may be left to wonder why their loss did not merit the same distinction. In fact, as many family members attest, neither the death penalty nor its alternatives can substitute for the tremendous loss of a loved one. A life sentence, on the other hand, does offer a sense of finality rendered relatively quickly, as well as an opportunity for some restitution or reconciliation in the future.

Marietta Jaeger's seven-year-old daughter, Susie, was kidnapped and murdered, but Marietta has never thought the death penalty offered any solace.

> The death penalty causes family members more pain than other senses. The continuous sequence of courtroom scenes inherent in death penalty cases only serves to keep emotional wounds raw and in pain for years. . . . Actually, the memory of the victim is grossly insulted by the premise that the death of one malfunctioning person will be a just retri-

bution for the inestimable loss of the beloved. In my case, my
own daughter was such a gift of joy and sweetness and
beauty that to kill someone in her name would have been to
violate and profane the goodness of her life; the idea is offen-
sive and repulsive to me.

In many ways of course, the death penalty is no benefit at
all; the threat of an execution means that there will almost
always be a lengthy trial and years of appeals. Over 40 percent
of death penalty cases are turned back for reconsideration. Once
a family becomes caught up in the quest for an execution, they
are likely to follow a path of disappointment and failure.

Many families of victims are totally opposed to the death
penalty. They echo the thoughts of Odine Stern, former director
of Parents of Murdered Children, that no sentences can ever
equate to the loss of your child's life and the horrors of murder.
Frequently, victims' families recognize that the death penalty will
inflict the same pain they have felt on the accused's family. As one
mother replied when asked at the funeral of her murdered son if
she wanted the death penalty, "No, there's been enough killing."

Murder Victims' Families for Reconciliation, another organization that deals with the grief of families, sponsored a major
national conference and educational program in June 1993
around the theme of moving from violence to healing. As an
organization, it is opposed to the death penalty. William Pelke,
one of the organizers of the conference and the grandson of a
murder victim, summed up his belief in alternative sentences.
"A simple life sentence without the possibility of parole can
ease the pain much sooner and enable the victim's family to
begin the process of healing. . . . As long as the thought remains
that justice has not yet been carried out, the healing process that
must take place is put on hold."

America may now be ready to abandon the death penalty. People strongly prefer alternative sentences to the death penalty once they are given the choice. The lengthy sentences that people prefer and that guarantee that convicted murderers will stay behind bars are now in place in almost every state in the country. To the extent that support for the death penalty continues, it is because the public in general, and jurors in capital cases in particular, are still unaware of this fundamental change in U.S. sentencing.

8

The Young Criminal Years
of the Violent Few*

Donna Martin Hamparian;
Joseph M. Davis, Ph.D.; Judith M. Jacobson;
Robert E. McGraw, Esq.;
and the Office of Juvenile Justice
and Delinquency Prevention

Juvenile delinquency is a serious phenomenon. It damages the victim, the social fabric of trust, and perhaps most of all, the individual delinquent. For the youthful law violator, delinquency is an omen of a bad future. Though we have seen that many delinquents for various reasons terminate their careers soon after they begin, we have also seen that there are many who persist. They will become recruits for the adult criminal population, with a potential for evermore destructive behavior and for costly dependency on the apparatus of corrections and welfare. The element of violence to which we have given attention heightens the gravity of their situation and emphasizes the urgent need for new and better solutions for the problems the delinquent presents. . . .

---

*Adapted from a pamphlet published in June 1985 by the Office of Juvenile Justice and Delinquency Prevention, U.S. Department of Justice.

During the late 1960s and 1970s, the juvenile justice system and, specifically, the juvenile courts came under increasing criticism. These criticisms resulted from several factors, including the escalation in violence committed by juveniles that increased 44 percent between 1969 and 1970; the growing public perception that the system was not working and that juveniles weren't being rehabilitated (although some have argued that the system wasn't adequately tested or funded, the public impression was that it had failed); perceptions that juveniles were being denied due process protection; and the fact that noncriminal offenders were frequently being punished more severely than serious juvenile offenders. In response to public concern and criticism, a series of changes addressed problems within the juvenile justice system. These changes included both closing or reducing the number of training schools in several states and adopting get-tough legislation in twenty-five states, which made it easier to try juveniles as adults for serious and violent crimes. In addition, Congress enacted the Juvenile Justice and Delinquency Prevention Act, which required the removal of noncriminal offenders from secure detention facilities and the separation of juveniles and adults in secure detention. Federal court action prevented the administrative transfer of delinquents to adult correction facilities. Some jurisdictions established procedures that ensured that only the most serious juvenile delinquents would be committed to training schools. . . .

A Brief Description of the Data and Research Methodology

This study is a cohort analysis, one of the very few attempted in the United States for the investigation of crime and delinquency. It is the only such study that focuses on a cohort of juveniles all of whom have been arrested for a violent offense, as opposed to a cohort of the general delinquent population. Also, it is the only cohort study to date that provides the "transitional" data needed to explore the continuity between juvenile violent offenders and adult offenders.

A cohort is a complete universe of persons defined by one or more events. Membership in the cohort of both *The Violent Few* (1978) and this study is defined by birth in the years 1956 to 1960, arrest for at least one violent offense as a juvenile in Columbus, Ohio, and residence in Franklin County, Ohio, during the course of the delinquent career.

The cohort consisted of 1,222 members, those identified in the original study plus 84 additional people. This analysis describes violent and other juvenile arrests in Columbus from 1962 to 1978, and follows the cohort members through their early adult careers, if any, up to mid-1983.

Cohort analyses are powerful tools for analyzing the relationships of age, race, sex, age of onset, progression, maturation, and termination of criminal behavior. They permit us to explore the issues of chronicity and severity, and to examine the effects of various dispositions on future behavior over time.

However, it should be noted that a cohort analysis is limited to a particular universe and generates authoritative propositions for that universe only. Distinguishing between the effects of history and maturation is often difficult, and gaps or losses of information may be introduced by the inability to obtain a complete data profile, either because the individual or the records cannot be located. Therefore, the interpretation of our findings should be approached with caution, and overgeneralizations should be avoided.

Juvenile and adult arrest records were obtained from the

Columbus Police Department, the Federal Bureau of Investigation and the Ohio Bureau of Criminal Identification and Investigation. Juvenile and adult corrections records were obtained from the Ohio Department of Youth Services and the Ohio Department of Rehabilitation and Corrections. Because more than 95 percent of the adult arrests of cohort members occurred in Ohio, as identified by the FBI, the corrections records of other states were not sought.

It also should be noted that the setting for the cohort in 1970 was a metropolitan area of about 750,000 people. The Columbus area was not characterized by high unemployment, extensive poverty, or juvenile gangs. In addition, the number of arrests for simple assaults was lower in the later years of the study than in earlier years, reflecting the police department's altered policy of handling many such cases without making a formal arrest or involving the courts.

The Juvenile Years: An Expanded Analysis of *The Violent Few*

The juvenile arrest records of the 1,222 members of our cohort reflect diverse patterns of criminal activity, ranging from murder and other violent offenses, to a broad variety of property and other nonviolent offenses. They provide a basis for several assertions about the character and distribution of their juvenile delinquent offenses.

1. *A relatively small number of violent juvenile offenders were responsible for most of the arrests.* The dominant population in our cohort is repeat and chronic juvenile offenders. Once arrested, the likelihood of a subsequent arrest was high. Sixty-

nine percent of those who had one arrest went on to a second arrest. Nearly one-third were chronic juvenile offenders, arrested more than five times, and almost three-quarters of those who had four arrests were on a fifth.

The chronic offenders arrested five or more times accounted for fully two-thirds of all reported delinquencies for the cohort, and the 105 youths with ten or more juvenile arrests accounted for more than one-quarter of all juvenile arrests. The juvenile chronic offender also accounted for four out of every ten juvenile arrests for index violence.

2. *Males and blacks are overrepresented in the cohort, and they account for an even greater proportion of juvenile crime.* Males accounted for 84.5 percent of the cohort, while blacks were represented by about three times their proportion in the general population, 54.2 percent. In addition, there were other differences between males and females and between blacks and whites. Most notably, females were less likely than males to be arrested for index violent crimes, and almost three-quarters of all the females were arrested for assault and battery as their most serious violent offense. Black youth tended to have their first arrest earlier than whites, were arrested for more index violent crimes, institutionalized more often, and detained longer. Blacks were more likely to be repeat offenders, while in percentage terms there were more white than black juvenile chronic offenders, that is, five or more arrests as juveniles.

3. *Violent juvenile offenders, as a group, do not specialize in the types of crimes they commit.* While public concern and the attention of policymakers have been focused in recent years on violent juvenile crime, our data suggest that violent offenses accounted for just over 30 percent of all juvenile arrests in the cohort. Most frequently, this violence is reflected in assaults,

37.4 percent; robbery, 25.1 percent; and aggravated robbery, 14.1 percent. Murder accounted for just 1.4 percent of violent juvenile arrests while rape and molesting accounted for 7.7 percent and 6.2 percent, respectively. About three out of every five of these arrests were for index violent crimes, while nearly 44 percent were for simple assault and molesting. . . .

4. *Relatively few violent juvenile offenders are repeat violent offenders.* Only 15.4 percent of the juveniles examined in this study have been arrested more than once for a violent crime, and fewer yet—8.1 percent—for index violence. . . .

Not all juvenile offenders go on to careers in adult crimes, and yet we know very little about the transition from the juvenile to the adult systems of justice. . . . Juveniles arrested for the first time at an early age, and who continue to be arrested throughout their juvenile years, are most likely to be rearrested at eighteen or nineteen years of age.

When not incarcerated, these persons remain active in the criminal justice system, at least to the termination point for our data collection. At every adult age, there is a small but consistent proportion who are not rearrested, but for the majority of offenders there is a continuity between the arrests of the juvenile and adult years. . . .

Policy Implications

At the outset, it was suggested that the findings set forth in this report provide a rather grim picture of our juvenile justice system and, more specifically, of the problems of violent juvenile crime. Yet, the data also yield new insights into the characteristics of juvenile and adult offenders, and valuable information about the development of criminal careers. As such, these data provide the foundation for developing more effective crime control, rehabilitation, and incapacitation programs.

Based on the findings summarized in this report it appears that most violent juvenile offenders make the transition to adult offenders; there is a continuity between juvenile and adult criminal careers; a relatively few chronic offenders are responsible for a disproportionate number of crimes; the frequency of arrests as adults declines with age; and incarceration has not slowed the rate of arrest—in fact, the subsequent rate of arrest increases after each incarceration.

Our findings permit us to address three policy issues:

1. *Should society's efforts be targeted at the problem of violent crime, or should they be designed to attack the persistence of chronic offenders?* It already has been suggested that our data provide no basis for predicting individual violence behavior. Only 15 percent of all juveniles arrested for a violent offense are arrested a second time for violence as juveniles. Most juveniles arrested for violent offenses are generalists who commit many more public order and property offenses than they do violent offenses. Juveniles arrested for violent offenses do not start with minor offenses and with each arrest increase the severity of the offense. In fact, our data indicate that violence is incidental in the chronic and violent offenders' delinquent and crime pattern.

The experience of the federal government's Violent Offender Program reinforces our findings. The program's inability to identify enough repeat violent juvenile offenders in several sites required changes in the definition of the violent offender. Only by modifying the definition of the target population were they able to identify a large enough population to carry out the program.

In contrast, our data clearly indicate that the chronic offender has a high probability of continuing to become involved in criminal activity. For this reason, the violent juvenile offender who is chronic should be the first priority of federal, state, and local officials. If we are to have a positive effect on juvenile delinquency, it will come from the recognition that most juvenile chronic offenders begin early, continue unabated except for interruptions for incarceration, and become adult offenders. And such a positive effect will come from strategies that let chronic offenders know that there are predictable consequences for their antisocial behavior.

2. *Given the continuous pattern of criminal behavior, why do we persist in treating sixteen- and seventeen-year-olds, and eighteen- and nineteen-year-olds in nonintegrated systems?* The decision to define seventeen-year-olds as juveniles and eighteen-year-olds as adults, the case in most states, is an arbitrary one. It causes us to treat sixteen- and seventeen-year-olds and those eighteen and nineteen in different systems, even though the sixteen- to seventeen-year-old juvenile offender may be more like the eighteen- or nineteen-year-old. Yet, there is no evidence to suggest that the criminal justice system would be more successful in dealing with sixteen- and seventeen-year-old youth, nor is there any reason to believe that the juvenile justice system could better handle the eighteen- and nineteen-year-old offender.

To be sure, the present dual system is not detouring criminal activity. It is essential, therefore, that we consider a variety of changes in court practices, in incarceration practices, and in both institutional and noninstitutional programs. Clearly, the answer here is not to toss the juvenile into the adult criminal justice system. The reforms of the past eighty years have been designed, in part, to limit this practice.

It may be appropriate, however, to consider the development of a variety of joint juvenile adult programs. These initiatives need to ensure continuity and accountability. They must give the juvenile justice and criminal justice systems incentive to try new approaches to deal with these persistent offenders. It is essential to find techniques to detour the delinquent and criminal activities that have been a major part of their juvenile and young adult years. . . .

3. *What, if anything, can we do to break the persistence of the violent and chronic offender?* Incarceration has long been viewed as the ultimate means of breaking the pattern of criminal behavior. Yet our data indicate that the institutional experience, for both juveniles and adults, did not have the desired effect. While generalizations are difficult, it is clear that few of our juvenile cohort members desisted after their day in court or a stay in a juvenile training school. This suggests that our juvenile justice system has little deterrent effect on future juvenile, and adult, misconduct.

What then, is the answer? First, it is important that intervention come early and that it not be nominal. To quote the authors of *The Violent Few*:

> Experience must not suggest that the system is aleatory. A youth must not conclude that the decision of the court depends on the mood of the judge, a special word from the probation officer, or his own neatly combed hair. He must expect that there will be intervention and that intervention will make requirements of him that he must meet.
>
> Such an intrusion into the delinquent's life need not be and usually should not be a term of residential treatment. It must not, however, be merely a scathing reprimand from the bench for supervision without supervisory contact. Where

violence was part of the offense, the youth in court should be impressed with the true seriousness of the situation. That impression must be reinforced by continuing encounters with representatives of the systems at school, in the home, and on the streets. Where appropriate, restitution should be required and where that is either impossible or inappropriate, a community order should be issued and enforced. Sometimes removal from a disorderly and delinquency-generating home may be needed, in which case placement in a foster home may be necessary.

In essence, the court system should be designed to ensure some degree of predictable graduated consequences for illegal acts. Individual conduct may not be predictable, but the justice system's response to criminal behavior must be.

. . . Finally, it must be recognized that some juvenile offenders cannot be kept out of trouble by any programs in operation today, or by any initiative envisioned in the foreseeable future. Nor is any single approach appropriate for all juvenile offenders. Yet, we need to develop new technologies and to assess new programs. And we must take actions, and modify existing programs, that offer substantial promise for a better life for our troubled youth.

PART TWO

JUVENILES AND THE DEATH PENALTY

9

Juveniles on Death Row: Case Profiles

Shirley Dicks

According to a report by Amnesty International, more than ninety juveniles have been sentenced to death in the United States since the death penalty was reinstated in the 1970s; all were aged between fifteen and seventeen at the time of the offense. Many have had their death-row sentences vacated as of July 1991, according to Amnesty International. Furthermore, although these youths represent only a small proportion of the more than twenty-four hundred prisoners under sentence of death in the United States, the United States has more juvenile offenders on death row than any other country known to Amnesty International.

The imposition of death sentences on juvenile offenders is in clear contravention of the international human rights standards outlined in numerous international instruments including the International Covenant on Civil and Political Rights and the United Nations. The execution of juvenile offenders is extremely rare. The more than seventy countries that retain the death penalty by law have abolished it for people under eigh-

117

teen at the time of the crime. The United States is one of only seven countries known to have carried out such executions in the last decade.

All those sentenced to death in the United States have been convicted of murder. Amnesty International does not argue that juveniles should not be held criminally liable or subjected to severe penalties where appropriate. However, international standards were developed in recognition of the fact that the death penalty, which denies any possibility of rehabilitation or reform, is a wholly inappropriate penalty for individuals who have not fully attained physical or emotional maturity at the time of their actions. A number of professional organizations in the United States, including the American Bar Association, are opposed to the execution of juveniles.

In the majority of cases examined, the prisoners appear to have come from particularly deprived or unstable family backgrounds. Many of them had been brought up in the absence of one or both parents; in many cases, the parents themselves had histories of alcoholism, mental illness, or other problems. At least twelve of the twenty-three prisoners had been seriously physically or sexually abused in childhood. Ten were known to have been taking alcohol and drugs regularly from an early age—as young as six in one case; others were under the influence of alcohol or drugs at the time of the crime.

There was evidence of mental illness or brain damage in at least fourteen cases. Six of these prisoners had long histories of psychiatric illness or mental disorders dating from early childhood. In other cases evidence of brain damage or mental illness was revealed in tests conducted during postconviction proceedings. Although the defendants had been found competent to stand trial, there was evidence suggesting that pretrial psychiatric evaluations were inadequate in a number of these cases.

Of fifteen cases about which Amnesty International had relevant information, eleven prisoners had an intelligence quotient (IQ) below 90 (a person of average intelligence has an IQ score of around 100). At least four individuals' scores fell within the borderline mentally retarded range and one other was significantly mentally retarded. Only two of the 15 had IQ scores above 100. Two of the defendants were illiterate at the time of their trials and learned to read and write only while on death row.

Most defendants were represented at trial by court-appointed attorneys or public defenders who sometimes spent little time preparing the case for trial. In at least nine cases, lawyers handling later appeals uncovered important mitigating evidence that had not been presented at the trial or sentencing hearing. These included cases where no information had been presented about the defendant's mental illness, mental retardation, or severe abuse in childhood, often because the trial attorneys had failed to conduct an adequate investigation into the defendant's background or psychiatric history.

In a number of cases the defendant's youth was not presented as a significant mitigating factor at the sentencing hearing or, if it was, this was rejected by the trial court. This appears to contravene the United States Supreme Court ruling in *Eddings* v. *Oklahoma* in which the Court held that the chronological age of a minor is itself a relevant mitigating factor of great importance.

The trial judge in a Florida case, for example, sentenced a sixteen-year-old offender to death on the basis that two aggravating circumstances outweighed the one mitigating circumstance to be considered, stating that age is a factor, when it is relevant to the defendant's mental and emotional maturity and his ability to take responsibility for his own actions and to appreciate the consequences following from them. He found that age was not relevant in this case as the defendant knew what he was doing, knew that it was wrong, and had tried to cover up his crime.

In some states minors charged with capital crimes are automatically tried in the adult criminal courts, which alone have the power to impose a death sentence. In these cases there is no individual assessment of the defendant's suitability to stand trial as an adult. In other states there must be a juvenile court hearing to decide whether or not to transfer the case to the jurisdiction of the criminal court. While the crime, record, and age of the defendant were taken into account in such cases, the defendant's individual maturity appeared to play no part in the decisions taken.

The most common ground for waiving juvenile-court jurisdiction in the cases examined was the lack of facilities within the juvenile justice system that could provide long-term custody, rather than a finding that the defendant could not be rehabilitated.

Case Profiles

Christopher Burger

Christopher Burger received a last-minute stay of execution in December 1990, pending an appeal regarding his mental competency. A decision by the United States Court of Appeals for the Eleventh Circuit was pending as of July 1, 1991.

Burger was convicted of the kidnapping, rape, and murder of Roger Honeycutt, a soldier who worked part time as a taxicab driver. Burger and an accomplice, twenty-year-old Thomas Stevens, were also soldiers in the U.S. Army at the time of the crime. Honeycutt was killed after Burger and Stevens had hired his taxi to take them to the airport to pick up another soldier, James Botsford. On the way to the airport, they forced the cab to stop and robbed Honeycutt of sixteen U.S. dollars. The driver was then forced into the back of the cab where Stevens sodomized him. Burger and Stevens picked Botsford up at the airport with Honeycutt tied up in the trunk of the car. They dropped Botsford off at the army base, after telling him what had happened and assuring him that Honeycutt would not be harmed. Burger and Stevens drove to a lake. Burger lifted the trunk to see if Honeycutt was all right, closed it again, started the car, and let it enter the water. Honeycutt died by drowning. Stevens was sentenced to death at a separate trial.

Burger and Stevens were each convicted on the basis of their confessions and the testimony of James Botsford. Each suggested that the other was more culpable. Burger said that he had thought they would abandon both the taxi and the driver after the robbery; he also said that Stevens had told him to drive the car into the pond. Burger's testimony was corroborated by Botsford, who testified at both trials that it was Stevens's idea to kill Honeycutt and that Burger had protested, saying they should let him go.

Burger's first death sentence was vacated and the case was remanded for a new sentencing hearing. At the new sentencing hearing in July 1979, Burger was again sentenced to death. The same court-appointed lawyer represented him at his trial and at the two sentencing hearings. No mitigating evidence at all was presented at either sentencing hearing. The jury heard nothing about the defendant's background. The trial lawyer later told an appeals court that he had felt that such testimony might be prejudicial to the defendant, as information given by relatives had suggested that he had a prior juvenile record.

A psychologist hired by the defense had conducted a brief examination of Burger before the trial and found that he had an IQ of 82 with a mental age of twelve. However, he was also of the opinion that Burger was a sociopath with a psychopathic personality. The lawyer therefore chose not to put the psychologist on the witness stand and the jury was not told that Burger had a low IQ, well below his chronological age. The lawyer also said later that he had been unwilling to ask for a full psychiatric evaluation of Burger as he did not trust the hospital that would have been assigned to carry out such an evaluation.

Burger's conviction and death sentence were upheld on direct appeal to the state courts. Lawyers then lodged a habeas corpus appeal on constitutional grounds. Two main issues were raised. There was a conflict of interest through the fact that Burger and Stevens had been represented by attorneys working for the same law firm, who had cooperated on both cases at the time of trial and direct appeal to the state courts. It was argued that this had adversely affected the handling of Burger's case, including the lawyer's ability to arrange a plea bargain. It was also claimed that Burger had received ineffective assistance of counsel, due to his lawyer's failure to investigate his background and present mitigating evidence at the sentencing hearing. New evidence was presented regarding Burger's troubled childhood, including affidavits from relatives and testimony given by his mother. The U.S. Court of Appeals denied the appeal, with one judge dissenting. An appeal was then lodged with the U.S. Supreme Court.

The U.S. Supreme Court denied Burger's appeal in a 5-4 majority decision in June 1987. The majority opinion found that there had been no conflict of interest arising from the partnership of Burger's attorney with the lawyer representing Stevens, noting inter alia that the defendants had been convicted at sep-

arate trials and that Burger's lesser culpability had been stren-
uously argued.

On the failure to present mitigating evidence, the majority
opinion acknowledged that the new evidence would have disclosed that the petitioner had an exceptionally unhappy and
unstable childhood, and that the record at the habeas corpus
hearing does suggest that the trial lawyer could well have made
a more thorough investigation than he did. However, they found
that there had been a reasonable strategic basis for the lawyer's
actions and that some of the new evidence might have affected
the jury adversely by revealing information about Burger's past
record and tendency toward violent outbursts.

In their dissenting opinions, four of the Supreme Court justices found that the trial lawyer had errcd in failing to present
any evidence at the sentencing hearing. The record indicated
that the lawyer's meetings with the defendant had been brief
and that Burger would have been unlikely to volunteer many of
the facts about his childhood. Burger's mother also testified that
she had spoken to the lawyer only after she had approached him
and that he did not explain to her the significance of the sentencing hearing or the need for mitigating evidence. The judges
found that the actual circumstances of the defendant's childhood, including beatings and his rejection by both estranged
parents and two stepfathers, would have been highly relevant at
the sentencing hearing.

The dissenting judges also found it unreasonable of the trial
attorney not to have sought information about Burger's background through fear that his past record might have been
revealed. They noted that the lawyer had not investigated
whether the defendant had a prior criminal record; in fact, the
record revealed nothing more than one incident of shoplifting
a candy bar and another incident involving an automobile. Jus-

tice Blackmun, writing the dissenting opinion, states: "The account provided by the petitioner's mother of petitioner's hitchhiking to Florida, to be with her after having been thrown out of his father's house and having to sell his shoes during the trip to get food . . . may well have outweighed the relevance of any earlier petty theft."

The dissenting judges were also critical of the trial lawyer's refusal to admit the testimony of the lawyer who had befriended Burger in childhood, who was willing to travel to Georgia at his own expense to testify at the trial, on the ground that he was black and that this may have adversely affected the jury. They were critical, too, of the trial lawyer's failure to ask the court for a full psychiatric evaluation of Burger. Justice Powell, writing the second dissenting opinion, noted that there was some indication that Burger may have suffered brain damage from beatings when he was younger.

Three of the Supreme Court judges also found that there had been a clear conflict of interest in the representation of the accused by lawyers who were partners in the same firm. They found that this may well have prevented Burger's lawyer from offering to have Burger testify for the state against Stevens in return for a reduced sentence.

In 1989, Burger was evaluated by Dorothy Lewis, professor of psychiatry at New York School of Medicine and a clinical psychiatrist at the Yale Child Study Center. She found that he suffered from organic brain impairment, probably from a series of brain injuries and the physical abuse he had received as a child. She found that he had sustained numerous severe traumata to the central nervous system, which had contributed to his early hyperactivity, his impulsivity, and his difficulty controlling his temper, and that he was mentally ill. She stated that the pretrial evaluation by the psychologist was highly inadequate and that his diagnosis of Burger as a psychopath or sociopath was contrary to accepted psychiatric practice, given his young age and history.

Christopher Burger was scheduled to be executed on December 18, 1990. He received a last-minute stay of execution pending an appeal on the question of his mental competency at the time of the crime in light of the later psychiatric evidence. Oral arguments were presented to the U.S. Court of Appeal for the Eleventh Circuit in June 1991.

Burger's parents married when his mother was fourteen, and his father sixteen. Chris was the second of four children his mother had borne by the age of twenty-two. His mother herself had been severely abused as a child and suffered from severe bouts of depression and mental illness, for which she was hospitalized during Burger's childhood. According to her own testimony at an appeal hearing, she often beat Burger as a child and sometimes had to lock him in a room to keep herself from harming him.

Burger's parents divorced when he was nine and he was placed in the custody of his father, who used to hit and punch him. He was unwanted by his father's new family and was sometimes shut out of the house. Chris was shuttled back and forth between both sets of parents and used to beg to be allowed to stay with his mother. However, at one stage he was left in the care of his mother's boyfriend for several months, during which period he was severely ill treated. During his childhood, his mother twice re-married. Burger was beaten by one of his stepfathers and also witnessed him beating his mother. Burger claimed that another stepfather had given drugs at an early age.

Burger received a series of head injuries during childhood, which rendered him unconscious on at least two occasions. He had learning difficulties at school and was hyperactive, a condition observed when he was at kindergarten, although no action was taken. At the age of eleven or twelve, he started to inhale organic solvents and to smoke marijuana. In 1975, when he was fifteen years old, he joined his mother in Florida, but this proved traumatic as she was at that time undergoing a divorce from her third husband. According to a report on the case, Burger attempted suicide with the help of his mother, who gave him six valium tablets that he consumed with whiskey. He was treated in an emergency medical room and released.

After being involved in a minor car accident in Florida, Burger was taken into custody by the juvenile authorities as his mother was unable to care for him. The authorities returned him to his father in Indiana. His father petitioned the juvenile court to take him but he was again released into the supervision of his father some months later. As soon as he turned seventeen, Burger's father signed permission for Chris to join the army. Burger was in the army for eight months before taking part in the crime for which he was sentenced to death. According to appeal documents, Burger's only previous record was one offense of shoplifting a candy bar, absence from school without permission, and involvement in a minor car wreck.

Janice Buttrum

Janice Buttrum's death sentence was vacated by an appeal court in 1989 after she had spent eight years on death row. She was resentenced to life imprisonment in June 1991. Janice was convicted of the murder of nineteen-year-old Demetra Faye Parker, who was stabbed to death and sexually assaulted in a motel room in Whitfield County, Georgia. Janice Buttrum, her twenty-eight-year-old husband, Danny, and their nineteen-month-old daughter had been staying at the motel at the time of the murder. Danny

Buttrum was also found guilty of the murder at a separate trial and sentenced to death. He later committed suicide in prison.

Several months before the trial, the defense asked the court for funds to permit them to hire a psychiatrist to examine Janice Buttrum, whom social workers estimated to have a mental age of twelve. The court denied this request but agreed to have her examined by two state psychologists. They later testified at a competency hearing that she was competent to stand trial. The defense called several lay witnesses who gave the opinion that she was not competent. After a brief deliberation, the jury found that Janice Buttrum was competent to stand trial.

The trial took place in Whitfield County, Georgia, after the defense unsuccessfully requested change of venue due to the extensive pretrial publicity the case had generated. In the year leading to the trial, Janice Buttrum had been described in numerous local newspapers as a bisexual sadist, with graphic accounts depicting the crime and her alleged role. Danny Buttrum's trial took place several months before Janice's own trial, and his had generated further publicity. The defense alleged that this made it impossible to obtain an impartial jury.

At the sentencing hearing, a private psychologist, Dr. Adams, appeared as the sole witness for the state. Although he had not interviewed Janice Buttrum in person, he testified that she was a sexual sadist, an antisocial personality type, and a paraphiliac who, he predicted, would commit other violent sexual acts in the future. Janice Buttrum had only one previous conviction for a minor offense, one not involving sexual violence. Dr. Adams said that he had formulated his professional opinion after reviewing materials given to him by the prosecutor, including the file from the Central State Hospital's competency evaluation. The defense was unable to call a rebuttal psychologist or psychiatrist because their renewed request for funds for a psychiatric evaluation had once again been denied by the trial court.

In seeking the death penalty, the prosecution alleged that Janice had been the dominant party in the crime and had directed her husband to kill the victim. The defense tried to rebut this theory at the sentencing hearing, pointing out that Danny Buttrum not only was eleven years older, but also had a prior criminal record, and was known to become violent when drunk. Janice Buttrum herself alleged that it had been Danny's idea to enter the victim's room on the night of the crime and that she had stabbed the victim in anger after seeing her husband having sex with her; she admitted that her conduct had been wrong, and that she deserved to be punished. She also testified that she had been frequently beaten by Danny. The defense also tried to introduce evidence from a social worker who said that Danny Buttrum had told her three years before the crime that he suffered from irresistible urges to rape women and had hostile feelings toward his mother, whom he had once tried to attack with a knife. However, the court did not allow this evidence to be presented.

The defense presented evidence of the defendant's acutely deprived background in mitigating against the death penalty after finding that the murder had been committed in the course of a rape and had involved torture, depravity of mind, and an aggravated assault to the victim.

Janice Buttrum's conviction and death sentence were upheld on direct appeal to the state courts. An appeal filed in the federal courts alleged that she had been denied a fair trial on a number of counts.

In September 1989, the district court upheld her conviction but vacated the death sentence on the ground that she had been denied the right to a fair sentencing hearing. The district court held, among other things, that the trial court had been wrong to deny the defendant funds for a psychiatric evaluation; that the testimony of Dr. Adams had been unreliable; that the trial court had been wrong to exclude evidence regarding Danny Buttrum's past urges to rape women; and that the prosecutor had made improper closing remarks to the jury when seeking the death penalty.

The State of Georgia appealed against the decision but it was upheld by the U.S. Court of Appeals. The case was remanded for a new sentencing hearing. In June 1991, the prosecutor agreed not to reseek the death penalty and Janice Buttrum was resentenced to life imprisonment.

Janice Buttrum was born to an unmarried mother who sold her at birth for the price of the hospital bill. Her early childhood was spent with childless foster parents who lived in a one-bedroom trailer. Social workers testified that the home was filthy and that the foster couple, who had drinking problems, failed to provide for Janice or to teach her basic hygiene. She regularly obtained her clothing from the town dump. For several years, her bedroom was a broken-down truck in the front yard of the trailer. She smelled and was ridiculed at school. An appeal document in Janice Buttrum's case states; "Several social workers and former teachers who had worked with hundreds of impoverished and neglected children testified that Janice was the most neglected child they had ever encountered."

During her early teens, Janice started to play truant and to run away from her foster home. She was befriended by an older man who, together with another man, sexually assaulted her. At age fourteen, she was declared a deprived child and placed in the custody of the county. She moved between one foster family and another. At one time she was placed in a youth detention center for six months, not for having committed a crime but because she had nowhere else to live. She met Danny Buttrum, who was twenty-six and divorced with two children, when she was fifteen, and they were married less than a month later.

At her trial, Janice testified that Danny often beat her when he was drunk and that on several occasions she tried to press charges against him, charges she later dropped. Evidence was also introduced that, despite the violence, she was obsessively devoted to her husband. At the time of the murder, Janice was pregnant and already had one child. Her second daughter was born in prison, two months before her trial. Janice had one prior conviction for simple battery.

Joseph John Cannon

Cannon's conviction and death sentence for the murder of Anne Walsh, white, in Bexar County, Texas, have been affirmed on direct and postconviction appeal. In July 1989, his lawyers requested a stay of execution on the grounds that Cannon was insane and incompetent to be executed. The trial judge ordered a psychiatric evaluation by two doctors. Psychiatric tests before and after his trial showed Cannon to be disturbed and immature for his age. He learned to read on death row. He has posed no behavioral problems in prison, but suffers visual hallucinations and depression requiring constant drug treatment. He has been taking Mellaril, an antidepressant drug, for most of his life.

Cannon had been thrown out of his home by his stepfather. He broke into an apartment and stayed there until he was arrested for burglary. The lawyer appointed to represent him on the burglary charge arranged for his release on parole, be-friended him, and invited him to stay with his sister, Anne Walsh. Cannon stayed about a week. Prior to her murder he had smoked marijuana, swallowed some twenty-five pills, and drunk a large quantity of whisky. Anne Walsh was shot several times in her house. After her murder, Cannon took about $100 and fled in the family's car, crashed it, and was arrested. He confessed, but he could not explain his actions. "I go crazy sometimes. . . . I had no grudge, or any reason to kill Anne; in fact she went out of her way to be nice to me."

At his first trial in 1980, Cannon pled not guilty by reason of insanity, but the jury rejected this and he was sentenced to death. The conviction was overturned in 1981. At his second trial in 1982, he pled not guilty. No psychiatric testimony or information about Cannon's highly disturbed background was presented. This was for tactical reasons because of the risk that such factors might be construed by the jury as aggravating rather than mitigating evidence. The jury was told only that Cannon was illiterate and aged seventeen at the time of the crime. He was again sentenced to death.

Three psychiatrists who examined Cannon in 1978 found him competent to stand trial. Tests revealed he had an IQ of 79, borderline mentally retarded. However, in July 1989, Cannon was examined again by two doctors who both queried his mental state at the time of the trial. One psychologist, Dr. Windel Dickerson, diagnosed organic brain syndrome and confirmed that Cannon had a subaverage IQ. He noted that Cannon's condition was certainly not of his own choosing, citing Cannon's learning disabilities, hyperactivity, head injuries, and the sexual abuse he had endured as a child. Dickerson found Cannon to have responded well to prison life. He had learned to read and write and was taking Bible classes by correspondence. "He has, in fact, done better than almost anyone . . . foresaw."

Dickerson concluded the prognosis of future dangerousness, presented to the jury at Cannon's trial, and medical testimony that Cannon could not be managed anywhere, was "wholly inconsistent with scientifically established knowledge and procedure." On the contrary, his IQ aptitude and self-image had all improved in prison.

Another psychologist, Jose Rodriguez, considered Cannon's case history exceptional in the extent of the brutality and abuse he had received as a child. Even in the worst of case histories, one seldom encounters traumatization as heinous and extreme as those to which Cannon was subjected to while growing up. Such was the depravity and oppressiveness of his upbringing that Cannon has thrived better on death row than he ever did in his home environment.

Joseph Cannon suffered from an extremely disturbed childhood. At the age of four he was hit by a pick-up truck and suffered a fractured skull, broken leg, and perforated lungs. He was in the hospital, and unconscious for part of that time, for eleven months. Upon his release, he was placed in an orphanage by his mother who was unable to care for him. Whereas before Cannon had been slow in his development, his head injury left him hyperactive. He suffered from a speech impediment and did not learn to speak clearly until he was six. He had learning disabilities, could not function in a classroom, and was expelled from school in first grade, receiving no other formal education. He sniffed glue and solvent, drank and sniffed gasoline, and at the age of ten, was diagnosed as suffering from organic brain damage caused by solvent abuse. He was diagnosed as schizophrenic and treated in mental and psychiatric hospitals from an early age.

Cannon was severely sexually abused by his stepfather, his mother's fourth husband, when he was seven and eight, and was sexually assaulted regularly by his grandfather between the ages of ten and seventeen. In one of his many psychiatric interviews Cannon told a doctor that he could not remember anything good that ever happened to him. He suffered from severe depression and had been treated with antidepressant drugs for most of his life. He attempted suicide at the age of fifteen by drinking insect spray. Cannon has a long and well-documented medical history of psychiatric disorders, yet attempts to have him committed to a state mental institution failed because of lengthy waiting lists.

Paula Cooper

On July 13, 1989, Paula Cooper's death sentence was set aside by the Indiana Supreme Court. The court held that because of her age at the time of the crime, the death sentence was a disproportionate punishment. She was resentenced to the maximum prison term permissible under Indiana law, sixty years. She must serve half her sentence before becoming eligible for parole.

Paula Cooper was convicted of the murder of Ruth Pelke, a seventy-eight-year-old white woman, who was stabbed to death in her home in Gary, Indiana. Paula Cooper and three other girls drank a bottle of wine before visiting Mrs. Pelke, a Bible teacher. She was stabbed more than thirty times with a butcher's knife. The girls stole $10 and Mrs Pelke's car and drove it until it ran out of gas.

Paula Cooper, the admitted ringleader of the group, pled guilty and was convicted without a jury trial in June 1986. On being sentenced she was reported to be the youngest woman to receive the death penalty in the United States this century. The other three girls, all teens of around the same age as Paula, received sentences of between twenty-five and sixty years' imprisonment for their part in the crime.

Paula Cooper was depicted by her defense as an abused child and chronic runaway. Her father beat her with belts and extension cords. She and her older sister were forced to watch him beating and raping their mother. On one occasion Paula's mother attempted to kill herself and her two daughters by putting them into the car in the garage and turning on the motor. Paula spent periods of time in foster homes and juvenile centers.

In its ruling in July 1989, the Indiana Supreme Court held Paula Cooper's death sentence to be unique and disproportionate in light of Indiana's 1987 law establishing sixteen as the minimum age for the imposition of the death penalty. Paula's death sentence provoked debate in the national and international media about the appropriateness of capital punishment for juvenile offenders.

An international campaign on behalf of Paula Cooper based in Italy brought her case to world attention. In September 1987, the pope urged Governor Robert Orr to grant clemency, and in March 1989, an Italian delegation presented to the United Nations a petition with one million signatures, protesting the death penalty and requesting clemency for Paula Cooper. Statements about the case were also made in the European Parliament's Political Affairs Committee.

Ruth Pelke's grandson, William Pelke, became convinced that his grandmother would not have wished her killer to be executed. "It was the Paula Coopers of this world my grandmother was trying to help." He befriended Paula Cooper, corresponds with her, and speaks publicly against the death penalty from the viewpoint of a family member of a murder victim. He, too, had urged that her death sentence be commuted.

James Terry Roach

James Roach was sentenced to death for the kidnapping, rape, and murder of Carlotta Hartness, aged fourteen, and the armed robbery and murder of her seventeen-year-old boyfriend,

Tommy Taylor. Both victims were white and from prominent families in the Columbia, South Carolina, area. On the day of the crime Terry Roach was in the company of a twenty-two-year-old soldier named Joseph Carl Shaw and Ronald Mahaffey, aged sixteen. All three had been consuming beer, marijuana, and other drugs. Shaw drove them to a baseball park northeast of the city. They stopped beside Taylor's car, demanded his wallet, and shot Taylor three times. They abducted Hartness who was raped and also shot to death.

The crime provoked enormous community outrage. After five days of intense investigation, Shaw, Roach, and Mahaffey were arrested. Mahaffey agreed to testify against the other two in exchange for a lighter sentence. The prosecutor sought the death penalty for Shaw and Roach.

Shaw and Roach waived their right to a jury trial and pled guilty. During a three-day sentencing hearing in December 1977, the judge considered mitigating factors for Roach, including his youthful age, lack of previous violent crimes, his emotional and mental condition, and his having acted under the domination of Shaw. The judge ruled that these mitigating factors were outweighed by the heinous nature of the crime. Roach and Shaw were both sentenced to death. Shaw was executed on January 11, 1985.

Roach was represented by a court-appointed attorney, Walter Brooks. A year before his representation of Roach, Brooks was charged in bar disciplinary proceedings with various irregularities in his law practice and with involvement in illegal drug trafficking. These charges were still pending when he represented Roach. Two years after Roach's trial, Brooks was disbarred from practicing law in South Carolina. However, his representation of Roach was found to have been constitutionally adequate.

The South Carolina Supreme Court unanimously affirmed

Roach's conviction and death sentence on May 28, 1979. Defense efforts on appeal resulted in some four postponements of Roach's execution date, but relief was denied in the state and federal courts.

As Roach's case received more and more statewide attention, South Carolina legislators introduced a bill to set the minimum age for the imposition of the death penalty at eighteen at the time of the crime. This bill was still pending when Roach was executed and its chances for passage died with him.

Lawyers representing Roach presented evidence indicating that he was borderline mentally retarded with an IQ of between 75 and 80. A neurological examination performed in 1979 suggested that he may have been suffering from the first stages of Huntington's chorea, a hereditary degenerative brain disease from which Roach's mother and several other family members suffered.

Shortly before Roach was executed he was examined by a neurologist who testified that he appeared to exhibit early clinical signs of Huntington's chorea, and that his social and criminal history may have been the early manifestations of the disease. A last-minute appeal to the United States Supreme Court for a stay of execution was rejected. Dissenting from the majority, Justice Thurgood Marshall expressed concern that Roach's mental condition raised substantial doubts whether Roach has any understanding that he is scheduled to die tomorrow. Five months later the Supreme Court ruled that the presently insane may not be executed.

Roach's lawyers also brought a complaint on his behalf to the Inter-American Commission on Human Rights (IACHR) on the grounds that his execution would violate United States obligations under international customary law and the human rights charter of the Organization of American States (OAS).

The IACHR appealed to the OAS authorities to grant a stay of execution; their request went unheeded.

Terry Roach was born into a poor white family in Seneca, South Carolina. His mother suffered from prolonged illness and his father, a truck driver, was frequently absent from home. Limited by his low IQ, Terry did not do well in school and left as soon as he could. He became involved in drugs and was placed for a while in a state reform school from which he escaped in 1977.

He found shelter in a rented house near Fort Jackson, South Carolina. The transient residents of the house were unemployable drop-outs involved in a variety of antisocial activities including extensive abuse of drugs. Some were considerably older and smarter than Roach, who easily fell under their domination. One of these men was twenty-two-year-old Joseph Shaw.

During his six years on death row, Roach's mental illness began to show itself as a result of Huntington's chorea and his mental condition deteriorated. A journalist who stayed with him in the last hours of his life described Terry Roach as a terrified, cornered human being who personified fear, not evil, and spoke with the simple words that a child would use. His lawyer described Roach in those hours as "very brave. He was limited and very slow, very concrete in his thinking. . . . It felt in some ways like sitting with a child who was about to have a really horrible dentist appointment."

Governor Dick Riley denied Roach's petition for clemency, ignoring appeals from Mother Teresa of India, former President Jimmy Carter, and the United Nations Secretary General Javier Perez de Cuellar. Terry Roach's last words, spoken from the electric chair, expressed his sympathy for the families of the murder victims. "My heart is still with you in your sorrow. May you forgive me just as I know that my Lord has done."

Heath Wilkins

Nancy Allen, a twenty-six-year-old mother of two, was working behind the counter of a convenience store. Wilkins and three other teenagers had planned the robbery of this store, which was owned by the victim and her husband. Wilkins and an accomplice, Patrick Stevens, entered the store while the two others waited nearby with a change of clothes. Wilkins first stabbed Nancy Allen while Stevens held her; then he stabbed her again seven times more while Stevens robbed the cash register. All four later divided the proceeds between them.

At the time of the murder, Wilkins was living rough in a local park with a girlfriend. The murder was carried out at around 10 P.M. Earlier that day Wilkins had drunk a quantity of alcohol and had taken three tabs of the drug LSD. He made no attempt to flee and was arrested two weeks after the crime.

Stevens pled guilty and was convicted of robbery and second-degree murder in the death of Nancy Allen. He was sentenced to life imprisonment, but will be eligible for parole in fifteen years. The third accomplice received a fifteen-year sentence, and the fourth was placed on probation.

Wilkins was transferred to the jurisdiction of the adult criminal court at a juvenile court hearing held only four days after his arrest, allowing little time for a court-appointed lawyer to investigate his background. After reviewing his juvenile record for offenses that included wrecking a tractor at age eight, various acts of theft, and starting fires, the court found that he was unamenable to treatment within the juvenile system. After the close of evidence, his lawyer requested and was denied a mental evaluation of Wilkins.

After the case was transferred to the adult court, the public defender appointed to represent him entered a plea of not guilty by reason of insanity. Wilkins was subsequently found competent to stand trial. State-appointed psychologist Dr. Mandracchia had examined him for one-and-a-half hours and, despite being aware of his long record of treatment in mental institutions dating back to the age of ten, the doctor found that Wilkins met the legal standard of competency. A second psychologist, Dr. Logan, appointed at the request of the defense, had found that the defendant was psychiatrically ill, but he could not provide a definite conclusion regarding the legal standard of competency.

Immediately after the competency hearing, Wilkins said he wished to change his plea to guilty and to waive his right to a lawyer and to a jury trial. After allowing him a week to reconsider, the court accepted his waiver of counsel. His former attorney told the court that there was much additional evidence regarding Wilkins's background and mental health than was contained in the competency reports. However, the court accepted Wilkins plea of guilty to first-degree murder on the basis of the competency decision.

At the sentencing hearing, both Wilkins and the state prosecutor asked for the death penalty. The state presented evidence of Wilkins's past record of juvenile offenses from age eight. Wilkins refused to present any mitigating evidence or to allow any references to his past mental treatment. The judge sentenced him to death on the basis of two statutory aggravating circumstances: that the murder was committed during the course of a robbery, and that it was outrageously or wantonly vile, horrible, or inhuman. The sentencing order made no reference to any mitigating factors found or considered by the court.

Wilkins took no steps to appeal, so the Missouri Supreme Court ordered a further competency hearing. Wilkins was examined by state psychiatrist Dr. Parwatiker, who concluded that he was not capable of waiving his constitutional right to counsel. A lawyer was then appointed to represent him. In September 1987, the Missouri Supreme Court affirmed his conviction and death sentence in a four-to-three decision.

In June 1988, lawyers filed a motion to vacate Wilkins's conviction and death sentence on the ground that he had been incompetent to plead his original trial and had received ineffective assistance of counsel. They also argued that to impose a death sentence on a sixteen-year-old offender was excessive and disproportionate. They presented new evidence showing that Wilkins had been severely abused as a child, in addition to his record showing severe mental disturbance and a history of mental illness within his family. At a hearing held in 1989 testimony was given by Dr Dorothy Lewis, professor of psychiatry at the New York University School of Medicine, and clinical professor at the Yale Child Study Center, Dr Jonathan Pincus, and Dr William O'Connor, a clinical psychologist and specialist in violent behavior. All three had conducted extensive examinations of Wilkins and had found him to be suffering from mental illness and incompetent to proceed at the time of his guilty plea. The state called Dr Mandracchia, who had made the original competency examination. Dr Mandracchia conducted a further examination and changed his testimony, concluding that Wilkins had almost certainly not been competent to plead or to waive his right to counsel.

The motion further alleged that the juvenile transfer hearing had been inadequate. Dr. Logan testified that, had he known the full facts about Wilkins's abused childhood, of which the juvenile services had also been unaware, he would have recommended a treatment program that may have changed the outcome of the transfer proceeding.

The court disregarded the above evidence and denied the motion on July 26, 1991. Records indicate that Wilkins had a chaotic upbringing and was badly beaten as a small child. His father left home when he was two and his mother suffered from bouts of extreme rage and depression, was regularly taking drugs, and according to her own testimony, administered severe beatings to Wilkins and his brother. Wilkins testified that his mother's brother had given him drugs, including amphetamines and marijuana, when he was six years old. Wilkins and his brother were also severely physically abused by their mother's boyfriend, who in addition to frequent beatings, often used to lock the boys in their room for hours on end so that they were forced to urinate and defecate there.

At the age of ten, Wilkins tried to kill his mother and her boyfriend by putting poison into Tylenol® capsules; they found out about it, emptied the capsules, and forced Wilkins to swallow them. Wilkins spent six months in the Tri Country Mental Health Center when he was ten years old and was described by a psychologist there as a severely depressed boy with a homicidal and suicidal ideation. Around that time, he had made the first of three suicide attempts by throwing himself off a bridge into the path of a truck; the vehicle managed to swerve, avoiding him. Intensive psychotherapy was recommended, but was never given. Wilkins spent the next three years in another youth center where he was placed on Mellaril and diagnosed as having a schizotypal personality. He twice attempted suicide by overdosing on drugs and alcohol. He was later placed on the tranquilizer Thorazine and was again placed in foster care. He then returned to his mother, who would not have him in the house. From May 1985 until the murder in July 1985, he was living on the streets.

Dalton Prejean

Dalton Prejean was convicted of the murder of a white police officer, Donald Cleveland, in Lafayette, Louisiana. Cleveland was shot when he stopped the car in which Prejean and three others were driving. All four occupants of the car had been drinking heavily and were under the influence of drugs. Dalton Prejean's brother, Joseph, was ordered out of the car and roughly searched. According to witnesses, Dalton believed his brother, whom he idolized was in danger; he panicked, took a gun from under the car seat, and shot Trooper Cleveland dead.

Dalton Prejean was represented by a court-appointed attorney and tried by an all-white jury after the judge changed the trial venue to a predominantly white area and the prosecutor then excluded all four prospective black jurors from the panel. Prejean was convicted of first degree murder on May 3, 1978, and the jury recommended a death sentence the same day.

Dalton's youth was not mentioned as a possible mitigating factor at the sentencing phase of the trial. Nor was the jury given adequate information about his state of extreme intoxication at the time of the crime. The jury did not learn about Prejean's childhood neglect and abuse, or about his documented history of mental illness and brain damage. It was argued on appeal that if the jury had known all relevant mitigating evidence, it is unlikely that they would have sentenced Prejean to death. This is borne out by the appeal for clemency made by one member of Dalton Prejean's jury shortly before the execution.

At his trial, Dalton was found to be borderline mentally retarded with a full scale IQ of 71. Tests performed in 1984 indicated that Prejean also suffered from organic brain damage that impaired his ability to control his impulses when under stress, and almost certainly contributed to his criminal behavior. Prejean was confined to various institutions between 1972 and 1976. Diagnosed as suffering from a number of mental problems, including schizophrenia and depression, he still responded well in the structured environment of the institution.

In 1974, aged fourteen, Dalton Prejean was committed to an institution after killing a taxi driver, a crime in which an older man was also involved. Medical specialists recommended that he required long-term medical in-patient hospitalization, under strict supervision, and that he would benefit from a secure and controlled environment. Despite their finding that Prejean was a definite danger to himself and others. he was released from the institution without supervision in 1977 because no more funding was available for his care. Six months later he killed Officer Cleveland.

Over the past century nine juvenile offenders have been executed in Louisiana, including Dalton Prejean. All nine were black males who were convicted of the murder of white victims, and all were convicted and sentenced to death by all-white juries.

Dalton Prejean was abandoned by his mother when he was two weeks old and was brought up by an alcoholic aunt in Houston, Texas. She was unpredictably violent and frequently beat him. Prejean was eleven when he learned that she was not his natural mother; this discovery caused him extreme emotional anguish and depression.

From his early childhood, he exhibited symptoms of paranoia and was sometimes violent. His family and acquaintances remember him as strange and crazy. He had few friends but was deeply attached to his older brother, Joseph. After his release from institutional care in 1977 he left Houston and moved to Lafayette to be near Joseph.

Dalton Prejean was the longest surviving inmate on Louisiana's death row. During his twelve years under sentence of death he received ten stays of execution. In interviews before his execution he expressed remorse for the crime and explained, "I've changed. There's a whole difference between seventeen and thirty." Referring to his nine-year-old son he said, "I think about Cleveland's children, the fact that they don't have a father either." And in his final statement Prejean again remembered the victim's family: "To the Cleveland family, they say it wasn't for the revenge, but it's hard for me to see, to understand . . . I hope they're happy."

On November 28, 1989, the Louisiana Board of Pardons recommended by a vote of three to two that the governor commute Dalton Prejean's sentence to life imprisonment without parole. The majority said they had been influenced by Prejean's childhood abuse, his mental deficiencies, his remorse, and his model behavior during his twelve years under sentence of death. On April 1990, the three board members who had recommended clemency again wrote to Governor Roemer to reiterate their special plea, that he review the case and reconsider his refusal to commute the death sentence. They said; "While we do not in any way wish to deprecate the seriousness of the crime, it was senseless and perpetrated upon one of the state's law enforcement officers, we feel that evidence deduced after the conviction suggests that Mr Prejean's sentence should be commuted to life without parole."

Shortly before Prejean was executed in May 1990, one of the original trial jurors came forward to appeal to Governor Roemer to grant clemency. The juror had recently received information that had not been given to the jury at the time of the trial. This led him to conclude that "I would, if I had the opportunity, vote against the death penalty in favor of institutionalization. I am entering my plea for a stay of execution and a reassessment of penalty." Under Louisiana law, the jury's vote for a death sentence must be unanimous. If even one juror disagrees, the sentence imposed is life imprisonment without parole.

The European Parliament passed a resolution on May 17, 1990, calling on Governor Roemer to commute Prejean's death sentence. The case aroused deep international concern and many hundreds of appeals for clemency were sent from around the world. Governor Roemer denied clemency on the grounds that the murder victim was a state trooper. "So on behalf of 780 state troopers, and thousands of police officers who put their lives on the line every day, the execution will proceed." Roemer and Prejean spoke by telephone on the night before the execution. It is understood that Prejean asked to have a chance at life and a chance to give something back to society, and that Roemer told Prejean his death was necessary to serve society.

David Tokman

David Tokman's death sentence was vacated in May 1988 on grounds of ineffective assistance of counsel. In March 1991, he was transferred from death row to Hinds County jail in Mississippi to await a new sentencing hearing, at which he could again be sentenced to death.

David Tokman was convicted of the murder of Albert Taylor, an elderly black taxidriver. The crime was committed with two accomplices—Michael Leatherwood, aged eighteen, and Jerry Fuson, aged twenty. All three were in the army at the time. According to the evidence presented at the trial, the three were traveling from their army unit in Louisiana to Jackson, Mississippi, to retrieve Fuson's car; they ran out of money and decided to rob and kill a taxi driver. Albert Taylor was killed by repeated blows to the head.

One of the co-accused, Michael Leatherwood, was also sentenced to death at a separate trial. However, his conviction was overturned on a point of law and he was retried and sentenced to life imprisonment. He was eligible for parole at the time of this writing. Jerry Fuson who had reportedly left the scene to retrieve his car while the murder was being carried out received a twenty-year sentence in return for testifying for the state.

The trial took place in Mississippi where Tokman, who was from Michigan, had no relatives or acquaintances. He was represented by a court-appointed attorney who met him for the first time several months before the trial but had very little contact with him thereafter. Not a single witness for the defense was presented at either the guilt or the penalty phase of the trial. Although the trial lawyer learned that accomplice Fuson was to testify as a key witness against Tokman, he did not interview him or any other state witness before the trial.

The state's evidence depended mainly on Fuson's testimony. Although he testified that he had not witnessed the actual killing, he said that it had gone ahead as planned, and that Leatherwood had tied a rope around the victim's neck and held him down while Tokman struck him with a knife. As no stab wounds or lacerations were found on the victim, the prosecution's theory was that Tokman had hit him with the blunt end of a folding knife. No murder weapon was produced in evidence. The state's case went largely unchallenged by the defense, who produced no evidence to rebut the prosecution's theory that Tokman, despite being the youngest, with no prior record of violence, was the most hardened and most culpable of the three accused.

The trial attorney later admitted at an appeal hearing that he had spent less than seven hours, including three hours spent drafting a court petition, preparing Tokman's case for trial and that he had not conducted any investigation into Tokman's background. A second lawyer he had hired to assist him a few days before the start of the trial had also spent little time on the case. Although Tokman had asked his lawyer at their initial meeting to contact his mother, this was done by telephone only after the trial had started. His mother then refused to travel to Mississippi to testify at the sentencing hearing, reportedly because she was unwell and was undergoing a difficult divorce. No attempt was made to contact any other relatives or acquaintances who might have presented mitigating testimony at the sentencing hearing. The defense counsel had planned to rely entirely on Tokman's own plea for mercy but chose not to put him on the stand when, the day before the hearing, he said he would ask for the death penalty.

Several months before the trial, the court had ordered a complete psychiatric evaluation of Tokman, including a battery of psychological tests, to assess his mental competency. These tests were never carried out, although they are normally administered during a competency examination. Instead, Tokman was interviewed by a state psychiatrist and psychologist for less than twenty minutes, during the course of which they questioned him in detail, without a lawyer present, about his involvement in the crime. His trial attorneys, who later stated that they were unaware of the court order, did not obtain a transcript of the state's psychiatric examination of Tokman. Nor did they arrange for him to have any further psychiatric examinations, even though they later admitted there was evidence to suggest that he had a death wish, had been abusing illegal substances, and had a poor relationship with his father. They later testified at an appeal hearing that their failure to obtain an independent psychiatric examination was not based on strategic considerations but on "lack of funds."

Tokman's conviction and death sentence were affirmed by the Mississippi Supreme Court in 1983. Two judges dissented and voted to reduce the sentence to life imprisonment, criticizing the absence of any evidence going to Tokman's rearing, training, or background. The United States Supreme Court declined to hear the case.

In October 1984, Tokman's appeal lawyers filed a motion for postconviction relief based on ineffective assistance of counsel. An evidentiary hearing was held before the circuit court in October 1986. Numerous relatives, acquaintances, and neighbors from Michigan testified for the first time about Tokman's background, including the fact that he had been neglected and physically abused by his father. His sister and others testified that, despite his unhappy home life, Tokman had been a hard working and considerate boy who had taken jobs from a very early age and did most of the housework because his mother was often out.

The appeal lawyers had also arranged for Tokman to be examined by two psychiatric experts who conducted extensive tests and reviewed his family history and background. Both testified at the hearing. Both concluded that the pretrial psychiatric assessment of Tokman by the state had been inadequate. Dr. Fox, a psychologist, also concluded that Tokman was intelligent but immature, with low self-esteem, and was easily led. He found that Tokman did not have an antisocial personality disorder and that he had a big potential for rehabilitation. Dr. Ritter, a psychiatrist, confirmed many of Dr. Fox's findings and testified that the defendant suffered the consequences of a deprived, detached, and lonesome existence in which he was rejected by his father; his mother was inconsistent; and he himself felt rather helpless, hopeless, and unloved. He stated that this created a tendency to be immature, basically dependent, unstable, and perhaps given to depressive episodes. The state presented three psychiatric experts who themselves confirmed some of the above findings. One state psychologist said that the defendant, like most adolescents, had some anti-social traits, but did not meet the full criteria for an antisocial personality disorder.

Following that psychiatric hearing, in May 1988, the circuit court vacated Tokman's death sentence on the ground that his trial attorney's conduct had fallen below reasonable standards and had prejudiced the outcome of the sentencing hearing. The court said that with timely investigation, mitigating evidence, which would have presented Tokman to the jury as a person other than the cold-blooded and callous murderer proffered by the state, could have been obtained and offered during the penalty stage. The State of Mississippi unsuccessfully appealed against this decision to the Mississippi Supreme Court. The Mississippi Supreme Court upheld the decision of the lower court in April 1990 and remanded the case for a new sentencing hearing.

In May 1990, Tokman's lawyers renewed an earlier appeal for a rehearing of their motion to vacate the conviction as well as the death sentence in the case. They argued that deficiencies by Tokman's defense attorney had prejudiced the fairness of the guilt stage of the trial. They cited, among other things, the lawyer's failure to interview any state witnesses, including Fuson, or to challenge inconsistencies in the evidence that had not established beyond doubt that it was Tokman who had killed the victim. They also claimed that the trial testimony from the victim's identical twin brother, although irrelevant to the question of guilt or innocence, had served to sway the jury emotionally; this same testimony had been specifically ex-cluded from the co-accused Leatherwood's trial.

Alternatively, the appeal asked the court to reduce the sen-tence to one of life imprisonment, instead of remanding the case for a new sentencing hearing at which the defendant might again be sentenced to death. They argued that this would be appropriate in view of his youth, the acknowledged deficiencies of his trial counsel, and the length of time he had already spent under sentence of death before his original sentence was vacated. This appeal was denied.

As noted at the evidentiary hearing in October 1986, the defendant came from an emotionally deprived and neglectful background. He suffered rejection by his father, who had been made to marry his mother when she became pregnant with him. According to testimony from relatives, his father abused him both verbally and physically, and frequently hit him with his fists and a belt, drawing blood on occasions. According to Tokman's appeal lawyers, at the time of his original trial his mother was impoverished, mentally unstable, and had emphysema. Despite his background, Tokman was described as a considerate and hard-working boy who had a high potential for rehabilitation. Tokman had no prior record of a violent offense.

Recent research indicates that, since the mid-seventeenth century, at least 286 children have been executed in the United States for crimes committed before the age of eighteen. This figure includes four juveniles executed since 1985 who were over eighteen by the time their executions were actually carried out.

United States law is based largely on the English common law system under which, in the past, an offender aged fourteen and over was automatically held to be criminally responsible for his or her actions and was tried and punished as an adult. Such children could be sentenced to death if convicted of a capital crime. A child from the age of seven to thirteen could also be tried and punished as an adult in certain circumstances and was also liable to the death penalty if convicted of a capital crime. Children under seven were held to be incapable of forming criminal intent. These basic principles continue in some form today, although most states have raised the minimum age and limited the number of offenses for which juveniles may be tried in the criminal courts. Some states no longer impose the death penalty on juvenile offenders.

Of fifteen thousand recorded executions in the United States only twelve have been carried out on offenders under the age of fourteen at the time of the crime. The youngest persons known to have been executed in U.S. history were three twelve year olds, two black slave boys and an American Indian convicted of killing a white man, who evaded arrest and was hanged years later by the federal government in 1885.

During the early twentieth century a juvenile justice system developed under United States law. This established separate courts for young offenders in which the emphasis was on rehabilitation and reform rather than punishment. All states and the federal jurisdiction today have a juvenile court system, and most retain jurisdiction over minors up to the age of eighteen. However, the laws of nearly all states allow minors charged with designated serious offenses, including capital crimes, to be transferred from the juvenile to the adult criminal courts. In such cases, minors have continued to be tried and punished as adults and to be liable to maximum penalties, including the death sentence where this is available. Some states have expressly excluded certain offenses from juvenile court jurisdiction; in others, the decision to try a juvenile in the criminal court for certain offenses is discretionary and usually takes place only after the juvenile court has waived jurisdiction in the case.

Most known executions of juvenile offenders have, in fact, been carried out this century under the above provisions. More than 190 of the 286 recorded juvenile executions in the United States have taken place since 1900. Juvenile executions, however, have always represented a small minority of between 1 percent and 4 percent of total United States executions. They reached a peak of 53 during the 1940s, but this was still only 4.1 percent of the total number of executions during this period. Executions of juveniles declined thereafter. Sixteen were carried out in the 1950s, and only three in the 1960s. James Echols, a black teenager executed in Texas in May 1964 for the rape of a white woman when he was seventeen, was the last juvenile offender put to death before the introduction of the present death penalty statutes. Twenty-one years were to elapse before another juvenile offender was executed.

On September 11, 1985, in Texas, Charles Rumbaugh became the first juvenile offender to be executed in the United States since 1964. Three further executions of juvenile offenders have taken place as of July 1, 1991: James Terry Roach, executed in South Carolina in January 1986; Jay Pinkerton, executed in Texas in May 1986; and Dalton Prejean, executed in Louisiana in May 1990.

According to data published by Professor Victor Streib in 1987, of all executed juvenile offenders since 1600 whose race was known 69 percent were black and only 25 percent were white. Streib found that racial disparities became even more marked after 1900 when the proportion of black children executed rose to 75 percent. He also noted that all forty-three rape cases resulting in the execution of juveniles up to 1964 involved black offenders. In contrast, according to Streib's data, only 9 percent of the victims in the cases of executed juvenile offenders were black, and this fell to only 4 percent between 1900 and 1986. Racial disparities based on the race of offender alone have fallen considerably under present statutes, although some 49 percent of the 31 juvenile offenders on death row as of July 1991 were black. Seventy-five percent had been convicted of murdering white victims. All four juveniles offenders executed since 1985, of whom three were white and one was black, had been convicted of crimes against white victims. Only nine of the juveniles were female. Eight of the girls were black and one was American Indian.

During the 1980s the U.S. Supreme Court was asked to rule on whether the execution of juveniles was permissible under the Constitution. Three key cases on this question have been decided since 1982 and are summarized here. In each case lawyers for the petitioners argued that evolving standards of decency made the execution of juvenile offenders cruel and unusual punishment, in violation of the Eighth and Fourteenth Amendments to the Constitution.

The Court was asked to rule on whether the infliction of the death penalty on a child who was sixteen at the time of the offense constituted cruel and unusual punishment. The petitioner was Monty Lee Eddings, who had been sentenced to death for the murder of a highway patrol officer when he was sixteen. This was the first time the U.S. Supreme Court had agreed to hear an appeal based solely on the defendant's age.

In a five-to-four decision given in January 1982, the Court failed to rule on the question whether the death penalty was per se cruel and unusual when imposed on a sixteen-year-old. Instead, it vacated Eddings's death sentence on the ground that the trial judge had refused to consider evidence of the prisoner's turbulent family history, of beatings by a harsh father, and of severe emotional disturbance as potentially mitigating factors at the sentencing hearing. These circumstances, the Court said, were particularly relevant when considered together with the defendant's youth. The decision affirmed the U.S. Supreme Court's ruling in *Lockett* v. *Ohio* that any aspect of a defendant's character or record presented in mitigation must be considered at the sentencing stage of a capital trial.

Although the Supreme Court did not address the constitutionality of the death penalty for juveniles, the decision is nevertheless important because it held that the chronological age of a minor is itself a relevant mitigating factor of great weight that must be considered at the sentencing hearing in a capital case. Writing for the majority, Justice Powell made the following observation:

> Youth is more than a chronological fact. It is a time and condition of life when a person may be most susceptible to influence and to psychological damage. Our history is replete with laws and judicial recognition that minors, especially in their earlier years, generally are less mature and responsible than adults. Particularly during the formative years of childhood and adolescence, minors often lack the experience, perspective, and judgment expected of adults. Even the normal sixteen-year-old customarily lacks the maturity of an adult. In this case Eddings was not a normal sixteen-year-old, he had been deprived of the care, concern and paternal attention that children deserve. . . . All of this does not suggest an absence of responsibility for the crime of murder. . . . Rather it is to say that just as the chronological age of a minor is itself a relevant mitigating factor of great weight, so must the background and mental and emotional development of a youthful defendant be duly considered in sentencing.

As in the past, only a small minority of death sentences imposed under present statutes have been for crimes committed by children under eighteen. Only 2.4 percent of persons sentenced to death in the United States between 1973 and May 1991 were juvenile offenders, with the number falling slightly to 2 percent since 1983. In 1990, the last full year at the time of writing, seven juvenile offenders were sentenced to death out of an annual total of between 250 and 300 death sentences.

A relatively large proportion of death sentences in juvenile cases have been reversed on appeal, thus reducing still further their number on death row at any given period. Although the adult death row population has increased by some 69 percent since the mid-1970s, the number of juveniles on death row has remained fairly constant: between around twenty-eight and thirty-five. As of May 1991, there were thirty-one juvenile offenders under sentence of death out of a total death row population of more than twenty-four hundred. Texas has the highest number of juvenile offenders on death row, seven on May 1991. This was followed by Alabama, with six, aged fifteen to seventeen.

Although death row conditions in the United States vary from state to state, they are generally extremely harsh. Unlike inmates in the general prison population, prisoners under sentence of death in most states have no access to prison work, vocational or training programs, or group educational classes. Inmates are typically confined for many hours a day, alone, in small, often poorly equipped cells. Although inmates may study individually, usually through the mail, for educational diplomas while on death row, the absence of training or educational programs together with long periods of cellular confinement and limited association with others appear to be especially unsuitable for juvenile offenders. Although rehabilitation is considered inapplicable to those under sentence of death, juvenile offenders have sometimes spent years in such conditions before having their death sentences reduced on appeal.

During 1986 and 1987, a team of psychiatrists and neurologists conducted a study of fourteen juveniles on death row in four U.S. states. The fourteen prisoners, who were chosen solely on the basis of their youth and not because the research team had any prior knowledge of their background, were interviewed at length and subjected to detailed psychiatric and neurological examinations. The researchers were surprised to find evidence of psychiatric illness or brain damage in nearly every case. Twelve of the fourteen had also been subjected to serious physical or sexual abuse in childhood.

The study's findings, which were published in the *American Journal of Psychiatry* in May 1988, included the following. All fourteen inmates had sustained head injuries as children, eight of which were serious enough to require hospitalization. Nine of the fourteen were found to have serious neurological abnormalities, including evidence of brain injury; seven suffered from serious psychiatric disturbances first manifested during early childhood and four other had histories consistent with severe mood disorders. Seven were psychotic at the time of evaluation or had been so diagnosed in early childhood. Only two of the fourteen had full-scale IQ scores above 90, with 100 being normal, and only three had average reading abilities; three had learned to read only since arriving on death row. Twelve had suffered serious physical abuse in childhood and five had been sodomized by older male relatives. Alcoholism, drug abuse, and psychiatric treatment were also prevalent in the histories of the inmates' parents.

Perhaps the team's most disturbing finding was that few of the cited circumstances had been brought to light during the prisoners' trials, despite being potentially mitigating factors against the death sentence. The team found that the prisoners and their families were reluctant to reveal details of abuse or mental illness, for example, and that the trial lawyers often lacked the expertise or resources to obtain the necessary clinical evaluations. Only five of the fourteen inmates had been given pretrial psychiatric evaluations, and these the research team found to have been perfunctory, providing inadequate and inaccurate information about the juveniles' disorders.

The researchers found that the juvenile offenders in the study were multiply handicapped not only through their natural immaturity, but also by additional factors such as brain damage or abusive family backgrounds. The report concluded that "juveniles accused of a capital offense are uniquely vulnerable; they lack the maturity or insight to recognize the importance of psychiatric or neurological symptoms to their defense; and they are dependent on family for assistance in a way that adult offenders are not. Our data shed light on some of the special difficulties encountered when adolescents are treated as though they were as responsible as adults and are condemned to death."

The fourteen prisoners in this study included all juvenile offenders on death row in the four states chosen: Florida, Georgia, Oklahoma, and Texas. Although the fourteen were not identified by name, some have since been identified through citing the study's findings in subsequent appeals, and several were among the cases reviewed by Amnesty International.

Public opinion in the United States may be said generally to favor retention of the death penalty. However, in an opinion poll conducted in Tennessee and Georgia in December 1985, more than two to one of those polled opposed the execution of juveniles who were under eighteen years old at the time of the crime.

10

An Attorney Decries Juvenile Executions

David Bruck*

Texas executed a prisoner named Charles Rumbaugh, Jr. Rumbaugh was the fortieth person to be put to death in the Southern states since the death penalty began its resurgence in earnest two years ago. By now, such executions are hardly news. Charles Rumbaugh was put to death for a crime that he committed when he was just seventeen years old. Until then, it had been more than twenty years since any American had been executed for a crime committed while he or she was a minor.

Charles Rumbaugh could not have been sentenced to death if he had committed his crime in South Africa, Libya, the Soviet Union, or China, instead of in Texas. The laws of each of those countries forbid the infliction of the death penalty on anyone who was under eighteen at the time of his crime. So does the International Covenant on Civil and Political Rights, which President Carter signed in 1978, but which the Senate has yet to ratify.

---

*David Bruck is a Columbia, South Carolina, attorney who specializes in death penalty cases.

The state of Texas uses sixteen as its age limit for the death penalty, and twenty-six other American states impose even lower age limitations—or no age limits at all—on who may be executed.

Rumbaugh was not the youngest person to be put to death in this century. That distinction belongs to a fourteen-year-old black boy named George Stinney, Jr., who was executed on June 16, 1944. Stinney was electrocuted less than two months after being convicted of the murder of an eleven-year-old white girl in Clarendon Country, South Carolina. At the time of his death, Stinney was 5 feet 1 inch tall and weighed ninety-five pounds.

George Stinney's case raised no great legal questions for the judicial system of that time. Indeed, it raised no legal questions at all, because his death sentence was never appealed to any court, and now the county court records of the case have been lost. Because it seemed safe to assume until recently that no one as young as Stinney could ever possibly be sentenced to death again in this country, there was little reason to recall the details of his obscure and long-forgotten case. But now that the United States has resumed executing people for crimes committed while they were juveniles, we might consider what, if anything, the crime and punishment of George Stinney, Jr., has to teach us now.

Betty June Binnicker and Mary Emma Thames, aged eleven and eight, had ridden Betty June's bicycle to the edge of the small lumber mill town of Alcolu, South Carolina, to pick wild flowers that spring afternoon. They didn't come home that night, and the next morning a search party of lumbermen found their bodies in a water-filled ditch. They had both been killed by blows to the head. Within a few hours, Stinney, the eldest child of a black sawmill worker, was arrested.

Eventually he confessed to having killed the girls and helped the police recover a railroad spike that, he said, had been the murder weapon. He was secreted out of the county just ahead of a lynching party of white lumber mill workers and merchants. That same day, the mill owner told Stinney's father to leave Alcolu, and Stinney's entire family left their company-owned home and boarded a northbound train with what they could carry, never to return.

Stinney was brought back to Clarendon County to stand trial on April 1944, just a month after his arrest. A special term of court had been summoned and the presiding judge had appointed a thirty-one-year-old local lawyer and fledgling politician named Charles Plowden as Stinney's defense counsel.

That spring, Plowden was preparing to run for the statehouse after losing a bid for the state senate in the previous election, and an appointment to so controversial a case could not have been welcomed. The case looked no easier after Plowden met his client; Stinney admitted his guilt, and Plowden saw no defense. He also decided that there was no need for a psychiatric evaluation and none was performed.

As the trial began, the Clarendon County Courthouse was overrun with a crowd estimated by the local newspaper at fifteen hundred, several times the capacity of the courtroom. The crowd overflowed into the hallway, down the stairs, and onto the courthouse grounds. Despite the huge crowd Plowden made no request to move the trial to another county, and a jury of twelve white men was selected before the midday recess. Testimony began at 2:30 that afternoon and by midday the prosecution had presented its entire case.

The main evidence against Stinney was his confession. According to the police, the boy had admitted that he'd seen the girls while he was minding the Stinney family cow, and that he'd followed them into the woods. Stinney admitted that he'd tried unsuccessfully to rape the older girl, and that he'd beaten both children with a railroad spike that had been lying near the track. The last piece of evidence presented was a birth certificate showing that Stinney had been born on October 21, 1929, and that he was therefore fourteen years old, the traditionally accepted age of criminal responsibility.

The defense offered no evidence. The local newspaper reporter described Stinney, who was dressed in a faded blue shirt and jeans, as looking unconcerned as he sat through the testimony. To Roston Stukes, a white Alcolu merchant who attended the trial, he looked more like he was scared to death. The boy looked like he was in a dazed condition, Stukes recalls. "He seemed like he didn't really realize the seriousness of the crime that he'd committed." The jury retired at five minutes before five in the afternoon to deliberate. Ten minutes later it returned with its verdict: guilty, with no recommendation of mercy.

According to the local newspaper reporter, Stinney was nervous and slightly excited when he was ordered to rise for sentencing. He bit his finger while he stood facing the judge. He had nothing to say. The judge sentenced him to be electrocuted at the state penitentiary in Columbia on June 16, 1944. The execution would have been automatically stayed for at least a year if Plowden had filed a one-sentence notice of appeal and then appealed the case to the state Supreme Court. But when Stinney was led out of the courtroom that Monday afternoon after the death sentence was imposed, he was on his own. Plowden never saw the boy from that moment on, never spoke to any member of his family, and never advised Stinney or his parents that he had a right to appeal.

There was nothing to appeal on, Plowden recalled in an interview given two years ago. And, he added, Stinney's fam-

ily had no money to pay for an appeal. With Plowden's withdrawal from Stinney's case, there was nothing left to do but
wait. The Stinney family had no resources or understanding of
the legal system; Stinney's younger sister Kathrine, now a
school teacher in Passaic, New Jersey, remembers that all her
mother could do during those weeks was pray. With no appeal
filed, only an order of clemency from Governor Olin D. Johnston could stop the execution.

Stinney's trial and sentence had attracted little attention
beyond Clarendon County, and none at all outside of South
Carolina. But as the date of his execution neared, Johnston
received pleas from several local National Association for the
Advancement of Colored People chapters, ministers' associations, and labor unions urging that George Stinney's sentence
be commuted to life on account of his age. Then, on June 12,
the Associated Press ran a story about the impending execution.
Several hundred letters and telegrams, the majority in support
of clemency, streamed in from throughout South Carolina and
the country.

A few supported the governor's announced intention to
allow the execution to proceed. Meanwhile Stinney waited in a
small holding cell just a few feet from the death chamber. On
June 13, prison officials interviewed Stinney in the presence of
a reporter for the Columbia *Record*. Stinney was reluctant to
speak at first, but he eventually repeated his confession. He also
told the officials that he had been finishing the seventh grade
when he'd been arrested. He appeared nervous when the subject of death was mentioned, the *Record* reporter observed.

At 11 o'clock on the evening of June 14, Johnston visited
Stinney in his cell. According to a newspaper report, Stinney
told the governor that at times his mind went blank. The following day, Johnston announced he would not grant clemency.

The next morning some thirty witnesses from Clarendon County arrived at the state prison to watch the execution. Just before Stinney was brought into the death chamber, the sheriff talked to the boy in his cell. James Gamble, the sheriff's seventeen-year-old son, was at the death house that morning with his father. Now a state police lieutenant, Gamble recalls that Stinney told the sheriff that he was sorry that he'd committed the crime, and that he hoped that God would forgive him, and that his parents would forgive him. Then it was time for Stinney to walk to the death chamber where the oak electric chair was waiting. A Bible, a gift from the sheriff, was tucked under his arm when he entered the room. According to the AP reporter, the guards had difficulty strapping the boy's slight form into the wooden chair built for adults. Another reporter noticed that young Stinney was such a small boy that it was difficult to attach the electrode to his right leg.

Stinney said nothing before the mask was lowered over his face. The *Record* reporter observed that after the first jolt of twenty-three hundred volts passed through the boys' body, the death mask slipped from his face and his eyes were open when two additional shots of fourteen hundred and five hundred volts followed.

James Gamble who stood next to his father during the execution remembers that moment. "His head went up and the mask came off his face, and I remember that saliva and all was coming out of his mouth, and tears from his eyes."

Gamble recalls how calm the boy had been when he'd been led into the execution chamber, as though, Gamble thought, he didn't fully understand what was happening to him. He was struck by the fact that Stinney appeared too small for the electric chair. "It had a lot of effect on me," the veteran state police lieutenant says now. "For a long time I turned against electrocution, period. I'm not that way today. I think the death penalty is proper in its place. . . . But I don't think a fourteen-year-old should be electrocuted. I didn't then, and I don't today."

Betty June Binnicker's father and older brother, Raymond, were also at the prison that morning to watch the execution. Both are dead now. Vermelle Tucker, Betty June's older sister, recalls that her father had looked forward to seeing Stinney die. But when her father and brother returned, neither of them was eager to talk about what he had seen, and Raymond refused to say anything at all.

No one quite as young as Stinney had been executed before in this century, and no one ever would be again. But executions of prisoners who were sixteen and seventeen at the time of their crimes continued until the mid-1960s. And now, with Charles Rumbaugh's execution in Texas they have resumed.

11

Juveniles on Death Row*

Victor Streib†

From an Interview with Victor Streib

I started working on the juvenile question in the mid '70s. I wrote a book called *Death Penalty for Juveniles* (Bloomington: Indiana University Press, 1987) on that topic, and since its publication, I've tried to keep my research up to date. Most of my present research and the book I'm writing now are on women on death row. I'm also an attorney and represent children and women on death row.

The number of persons currently under juvenile death sentences has dropped to the lowest point since 1983, when I first began recording the data. As of February 1989, twenty-seven

---

*Reprinted from *Congregation of the Condemned: Voices Against the Death Penalty,* edited by Shirley Dicks (Amherst, N.Y.: Prometheus Books, 1991), pp. 191–98.

†Victor Streib is a professor of law at Cleveland State University in Ohio.

167

persons were on death row for crimes committed while under the age of eighteen, the most typical age cutoff for juvenile court. These twenty-seven condemned juveniles constitute only 1.2 percent of the total number of persons on death row.

Most of these kids have had a difficult background. Dorothy Lewis has researched this subject and found that almost all of those on death row came from very abusive homes.* But there are some who did not come from such a background and whose homelife was generally good. I think the problem is not that they come from single-parent families, or that they're poor, but that they've seen violence in their families. They get the message very clearly that violence is the way to solve problems. Then when they are confronted by their own problems, they resort to violence.

Almost all of the juveniles on death row have had court-appointed attorneys. They had public defenders at trial, and when they are put on death row, they have to get an attorney to handle the appeals. In most of the states, the public defender cannot take the case beyond the trial level. They have to get a new attorney for the state appeal, and after the state appeal is through, and they're getting ready to go on into federal courts, then the state public defender can't work for them any longer. The state-paid public defenders are not allowed to represent anyone in anything other than a state action. Trying to find lawyers to represent them in federal action is very hard to do. So they are often left without any lawyer at all.

I think all of the twenty-seven kids now on death row have a lawyer. But a good number of the two thousand adults on

*See Dorothy O. Lewis, *Vulnerabilities to Delinquency* (New York: Luce, 1981), and Dorothy O. Lewis and David A. Balla, *Delinquency and Psychopathology* (New York: Grune, 1976).

death row do not have an attorney and could go all the way to execution without one.

The most serious problem is at the trial when they are appointed public defenders. The public defender, while he usually is a very competent attorney, has a big case load and not much experience in death-penalty cases. I think they often don't do as good a job as one would hope they would do at the trial level. By the time they get to the appeal level, if the trial hasn't been conducted in all the right ways, then it's hard to get relief.

There is an enormous amount of pressure on these attorneys. They have a huge case load, so they don't have as much time to devote to public-defender cases as they ought to, and there is a lot of political pressure in these cases. If an attorney takes a murder case in his home town and is representing somebody whom the press is hounding every day, and the politicians are making speeches about, it is pretty tough to practice law in that community. He's going to hurt his law practice and is going to make all his present clients angry; even his kids are going to get shouted at at school.

There's an enormous amount of difficulty for local attorneys to take local cases because they're sensationalized by the press and they make the attorney out to be some kind of monster, and it's just very difficult to deal with. It's easier for someone from out of state to come in and do the job. He's not going to care if anyone in the town likes him or not. He can leave and go home and nobody knows what he's been doing or who he's been defending.

The political pressures are really enormous for these attorneys and I really feel for them. They have to make a living and they have to live in their communities; so, while I criticize the general level of representation these kids are getting, I have to understand the difficulties these attorneys are facing.

We have fourteen states that have juveniles on death row at the present time. Only three of them have been executed since the death penalty has been reinstated. One was in South Carolina and the other two were in Texas. These were all seventeen-year-olds and they were executed in 1985 and 1986.

Charles Rumbaugh was born on June 23, 1957, one of several children in the west-Texas, white, Catholic family of Harvey and Rebecca Rumbaugh. Raised in a constantly moving family with a violent, alcoholic father, Rumbaugh committed his first serious offense when he broke into a schoolhouse at age six. At seven he was wild and uncontrollable. At thirteen he was placed in reform school. He spent the next four years there, fulfilling his ambition to learn how to commit more and better crimes. In Rumbaugh's own words, the Texas juvenile justice system "took a 13-year-old boy and turned out a hardened criminal."

Once released he began his life of crime in earnest. Soon he was in a mental hospital for treatment of manic depression. He escaped from the hospital early in 1975 and continued his life of crime. He decided to commit his next robbery at a small jewelry store. He pointed the gun at the jeweler and demanded money, but the jeweler resisted and reached for his own gun. They struggled and Rumbaugh got the better of him. He shot twice and killed him.

Police questioned Rumbaugh and he provided them with a written confession. He was tried and found guilty of murder and robbery, and was sentenced to death.

Rumbaugh seemed resigned to his death sentence. In a letter he wrote:

If they were to come to my cell and tell me I was going to be executed tomorrow, I would feel relieved, in a way. The waiting would be over. I would know what to expect. To me, the dying part is easy; it's the waiting and not knowing that's hard. I feel like I have been traveling down a long and winding tunnel for the past nine years, the length of time I have been on death row, and now I can see no end to the tunnel, no light at the end of it, just more long years of the same. I have reached the point where I no longer really care. . . . I'm so damn tired and disgusted with sitting here and watching my friends take that final trip to the execution chamber, one after the other, while I continue to wait and speculate about when my time will come. They're killing me a little bit each day.

The day before his execution Rumbaugh was visited by friends he had corresponded with over the years, and by three sisters and a brother-in-law. His mother went to the prison but at the last minute decided not to see him. Shortly after midnight, Rumbaugh faced his execution calmly. He refused communion and requested that no religious persons be with him at his death. He gave a last statement to the witnesses at his execution. "About all I can say is goodbye. For the rest of you, even though you don't forgive me my transgressions, I forgive you for yours against me. That's all I wish to say. I'm ready to begin my journey."

He was the first person to be put to death for a crime committed while under age eighteen in the post-Furman era of capital punishment. Was he deterred by the death penalty? "I was seventeen years old when I committed the offense for which I am about to die, and I didn't even start thinking and caring about my life until I was at least twenty."

Juveniles generally don't get treated as harshly as adults regardless of what they do. That's the reason we have juvenile courts, to take care of that. There is a principle in our law that assumes juveniles can't commit horrible acts and do serious harm to people. They are not held fully accountable for what they do. I think it's surprising that some actually do get the death sentence; they're the cases that slipped through the cracks, so to speak, or were treated strangely. I think it's fair to say that these are exceptional cases, and they are hard to explain because they are so very rare. They aren't the worst killers by any means, they aren't the worst kids, and they aren't necessarily in the same towns or the same states.

The death penalty for juveniles is gradually disappearing in most states, as it did in Tennessee. Most states are passing minimum-age laws for the death penalty, which stipulate that, no matter what the crime, if you're under a certain age, you can't get the death penalty. That's been going on since 1980. Even the states that want the death penalty don't want to see it applied to juveniles. Moreover, in the states that have no minimum-age provision in their death-penalty laws, the judges and juries have been reluctant to give the death sentence to a juvenile. It used to be that fifteen or twenty juveniles were sentenced to death a year, and now it's only two or three.

For the worst offenses by children, legal processes have been followed for more than a century that are markedly less harsh and punitive than those for similar offenses by adults. Attempts are made to protect children during legal proceedings and to impose nonpunitive, treatment-oriented sanctions on them for their offenses. Retribution and deterrence, the age-old justifications for adult criminal sanctions, have only recently made minor inroads into the practice of juvenile corrections. Even though juveniles, just like adults, sometimes commit horrible offenses and sometimes suffer horrible abuses, juvenile offenders and victims are legally, socially, and politically different.

In this century, the youngest person to be executed was fourteen, in South Carolina. His case has gotten a lot of attention because he was so very young. He was really just a little kid and was so small he didn't fit in the electric chair. They had to adjust the straps to make him fit and his feet still dangled.

From *Death Penalty for Juveniles*

Leaders in the legal, criminological, and social-policy fields almost universally oppose the death sentence for juveniles. The prestigious American Law Institute excluded the death penalty for crimes committed while under age eighteen from its influential Model Penal Code, concluding that "civilized societies will not tolerate the spectacle of execution of children." This position was also adopted by the National Commission on Reform of Criminal Law.

In August of 1983, the American Bar Association adopted as its formal policy a resolution stating that the association "opposes, in principle, the imposition of capital punishment upon any person for any offense committed while under the age of eighteen." That was the first time in the history of the organization that it took a formal position on any aspect of capital punishment. The *Washington Post* endorsed the ABA's policy and urged it as a minimum requirement for jurisdictions having capital punishment.

All European countries forbid the death penalty for crimes committed while under age eighteen. More than three-fourths of the nations of the world have set eighteen as the minimum age for the death penalty. The United Nations endorsed this position in 1976. Another indication of the present global attitude is the condemnation of the death penalty by Pope John

Paul II, the first such position by any pope in history. Even in time of war, the Geneva Convention prohibits execution of civilians under age eighteen at the time of offense.

If the number of juveniles selected for death sentencing and possible execution is only a tiny portion of the number of juveniles who commit capital crimes, how are they selected? In an analysis of the cases of the eleven adults selected for execution from 1977 through 1983, the conclusion was that they were not unique and no rational basis could be discerned for their resulting in execution. Justice Brennan concluded that these adult executions were not "selected on a basis that is neither arbitrary nor capricious, under any meaningful definition of those terms." Extrapolating from these conclusions about adult executions, the inference seems much stronger in the matter of juvenile death sentences and executions. Their even rarer and more random pattern of occurrence leaves no alternative to the conclusion that they are most freakishly imposed. No rational selection process can be determined, and one is left to conclude that the basis of selection is arbitrary and capricious.

Does the Eighth Amendment prohibit the death penalty for crimes committed while under age eighteen? The Supreme Court has avoided giving a direct answer to this question but has provided a general analytical framework from which answers may be derived. The foregoing analysis suggests that the most persuasive answer, given this general analytical framework, is yes—the death penalty for juveniles is cruel and unusual under the Eighth Amendment. This answer follows from a step-by-step consideration of the supporting arguments for the death penalty as they apply to adolescents. In this application, the force of these supporting arguments either disappears or in some cases suggests that the threat of the death penalty may become an attraction to death-defying adolescents. The line should be drawn at age eighteen, since that is by far the most common age for similar restrictions and limitations. This line should emanate from the Eighth Amendment and should be imposed by the Supreme Court.

Indications of a trend seem to be appearing. More and more state legislatures, trial courts, and appellate courts are excluding juveniles from the death penalty. Specific provisions are appearing in statutes recently amended by legislatures. Trial courts, even when they are authorized to sentence juveniles to death, are very rarely doing so. Appellate courts are finding a variety of reasons to reduce the death penalties of juveniles without imposing a blanket prohibition on all such sentences. State laws seem to be moving, however gradually, away from the death penalty for juveniles.

While some persons have been executed for crimes committed as young as age ten, most of the juvenile offenders were age sixteen or seventeen when they committed their crimes; the average age was just over sixteen years. The younger offenders, particularly those under age fourteen, were executed in greatest numbers before 1900. That is also true of the nine female juveniles executed. The last juvenile executed was in 1912.

In line with the historical pattern for all executions in this country, the southern states predominate in juvenile executions, with 65 percent of the total. Georgia is the leader, with forty-one juvenile executions. Other leading states are North Carolina, Ohio, New York, Texas, and Virginia. Thirty-five states and the federal government have executed juveniles for their crimes.

This summary of the characteristics of these executed children and their crimes raises more questions than it answers. But perhaps it will at least serve to refute the commonly held belief that the death penalty has always been reserved for our most hardened criminals, and middle-aged three-time losers. While they are often the ones executed, offenders of more tender years, down even to prepubescence, also have been killed lawfully, hanging from our gallows, restrained in our gas chambers, sitting in our electric chairs, and lying on our hospital gurneys.

If we discard the death sentence for juveniles, what can be done about violent juvenile crime? Many persons support the death penalty for juveniles from fear of and outrage over violent juvenile crime. This fear and outrage are shared by all reasonable persons, whether they are for or against the death penalty. Two answers to this problem suggest themselves. The temporary solution is to impose long-term prison sentences on such violent juveniles. That would ensure that they were reasonably mature adults and had been subjected to whatever rehabilitative programs were available before they were set free again. Life imprisonment without possibility of parole seems an unwise choice, like any personal or business decision that we vow never to reconsider regardless of future events. Few of the violent juveniles would be good candidates for parole in less than ten or twenty years, but that option should be left open for them to work toward.

Unfortunately, no one yet has the cure for violent juvenile crime. It seems clear, however, that the death penalty for juveniles has been given a long trial period and has been found wanting. It's societal costs are enormous, and it delays our search for a rational and acceptable means of reducing violent juvenile crime.

12

Who's to Blame?

Ward Weaver, Jr.

A baby boy is born to a family and the first toy the father buys him is a toy gun. The child starts to walk and play with the gun, pointing it at mommy and daddy saying, "Bang, bang, you're dead." And the parents reply, "How cute."

The child gets a little older and starts playing cowboys and Indians, cops and robbers, and war with the neighbor boy, and every time he shoots the neighbor boy dead, a few minutes later, the neighbor boy gets up and they start all over again.

The child gets a little older and the father starts teaching him how to shoot real guns and takes him hunting, introduces him to real killing, and justifies it as getting food for the family. If the child misses his shot, he is made fun of by everyone the father can tell, but if the boy shoots straight and true, making a clean kill, he is praised by the same people that would otherwise make fun of him.

When a little older, the same child goes into the service and from the time he is woken up till the time he falls asleep at night, he eats, breathes, and thinks about nothing else but KILL,

177

KILL, KILL. And if he doesn't he is punished every moment he doesn't. Then he goes to war and does what he is trained to do, KILL.

Then he comes home and all he is told before being released to go home is, "You're home now, so forget everything you have been doing up till now."

He goes home and for a while everything runs somewhat smoothly. In all situations he tries to forget, but is reminded almost every day of his past. And then one day it happens. Whether it is due to drugs, posttraumatic stress, overwork, depression, or a number of other things, or a combination of two or more of these, he kills someone.

Now the same people that praised him want to kill him. WHO'S TO BLAME?

Life on death row for me is long days of hoping that night won't come too soon and when it does, trying to keep occupied so sleep is kept to a minimum. Afraid of nightmares, afraid of twenty-some years, afraid as well of flashes of things you are accused of being on death row for. Hours are spent trying to figure out what happened and why.

You hold on to the memories of the fun things you did in the past and in your mind relive those moments over and over, a thousand times each year. You try not to think of what life might have been if you were still out on the streets.

If you have a television, you try not to watch programs that have happy endings for they make you cry and you wonder why that is, for things like that didn't affect you before. You find yourself watching programs but when there is killing going on you change channels to keep your insides from tearing you apart. For they cause more flashbacks than anything. You can't watch war movies for even though you know it is only Hollywood, your feelings and tears don't know the difference. You sit every day knowing you're going to die and there is very little hope that will change.

Every day you watch people on television protesting against abortion, the killing overseas, and yet, these are the same people that want executions done at home; want violence done away with, yet will hurt, even kill, people who don't believe the same as they do. I have seen people who voted the death penalty in who, when one of their children fall prey to the law, say it is a bad law and should be changed.

People believe everything they read in the newspapers and see on the television news, for they believe that if it is in print or on the tube, it has to be true. They believe that cops do no wrong, and when one of them does, reply, "Oh, that is just one incident." How many does it take to show that the law is as corrupt as anything else, for no matter what you belong to, you are first and foremost, HUMAN. Humans are taught from birth by their peers to hurt and kill.

13

Gary Graham
Juvenile on Death Row

Shirley Dicks

Gary Graham is a young African-American who is on death row for the murder of Bobby Grant Lambert, a fifty-three-year-old white man who was shot in the parking lot of a Houston grocery store on May 13, 1981. On two separate occasions, Gary has been spared from execution by eleventh-hour reprieves. Gary has always maintained his innocence and was convicted solely on the basis of the highly questionable identification by a single witness. No other physical or circumstantial evidence connected Gary to the crime, and three other eyewitnesses could not identify Gary.

Gary was seventeen years old at the time of the murder. There are three men on death row from Harris County, Texas, who were seventeen at the time of the offenses for which they were sentenced to death. All three are African-American.

At approximately 9:30 P.M. on the night of the crime, Lambert purchased about $20 worth of items at the Safeway store. He paid with a $100 bill and received change. As he walked across the lot to his car, one witness said a man came up from behind, pointed a gun at him, and after a brief confrontation, shot Lambert. The gunman fled. Lambert had sixty $100 bills on his person. The $70 plus in change from his purchase was not found. Several individuals witnessed the crime.

The witness closest to the crime was Daniel Grady, who was sitting in his parked car. The altercation took place approximately three steps in front of his car. Grady testified that the black man who shot Lambert was facing the car during the altercation and he could see the gunman's face. Lambert fell upon Grady's car after the shooting. Grady was unable to identify Gary as the person he saw shoot Lambert.

Another witness was Wilma Amos, a patron of the store. While shopping in the store, she talked extensively with Lambert and saw him several different times in the store. She also testified that she saw another man in the store who drew her attention. She described him as a black man wearing black pants and a white jacket. Amos also saw this man several times, looking at Lambert, walking slowly and not buying anything. Amos was in the parking lot walking to her van when she witnessed the altercation and the shooting.

After the shooting, the gunman walked towards Amos as he was leaving the parking lot and stopped in front of her, facing her from a distance of about four feet. Amos, who is five feet two inches tall, remembers the gunman was practically eye to eye with her, that he was only slightly taller. She could not identify Gary as the man she saw shoot Lambert and has since categorically stated that Gary Graham was not the gunman.

Bernadine Skillern was sitting in a car on the parking lot with two of her children sitting in the backseat at the time of the shooting. She estimated that she was thirty-three to forty-four feet away from the Grady car when the shooting occurred, and she only saw the gunman briefly from the side. She blew her horn and the shooter looked at the car. Skillern testified that she saw his face for a split second.

Nearly two weeks later, on May 26, Skillern was shown five photographs by police detectives. Gary was in jail at the time on other unrelated charges and his photograph was among those shown to Skillern. She was unable to make an identification from the photographs. The next day Skillern was taken to a lineup and identified Gary. Gary was the only person included in both the photo array and the live lineup.

After Skillern's identification, Gary was charged with the capital murder of Lambert. Gary confessed to a series of crimes committed between May 14 and May 21, however, he has always maintained his innocence in the Lambert shooting. Gary was tried for capital murder in state district court in Houston in October 1981. Bernadine Skillern's identification was the only evidence connecting Gary to the crime. No other witness to the crime was able to identify the gunman, not the witness closest to the crime, nor the witness who had observed the two individuals involved for the longest time.

No other evidence, no fingerprints, no ballistics, and no informant linked Gary Graham to the murder. Although police recovered a gun that Gary had used in one of the crimes to which he confessed, there was no evidence connecting that gun to the shooting of Lambert. In fact, a ballistics test conducted by the Houston police showed conclusively that the bullet that killed Lambert was not fired from the gun that was taken when Gary was arrested.

Gary was represented by a court-appointed attorney. The attorney's investigator has sworn in an affidavit that the attorney insinuated that Gary was guilty, and as a result a complete pretrial investigation was not conducted. The investigator, Merv West, confirms that Gary provided his attorney with a list of alibi witnesses. Neither the investigator nor the attorney interviewed the alibi witness. Only two crime scene witnesses were interviewed.

At least four other crime scene witnesses were available who were not called to testify in court. All the crime scene witnesses, with the exception of Bernadine Skillern, described the gunman as being approximately five feet five inches tall. At the time of the murder Gary was five feet nine inches tall.

Ronald Hubbard was a store employee who was on the parking lot gathering shopping carts when the shooting occurred. Hubbard told police that the gunman was about five feet five inches tall. He was shown a live lineup that included Gary—the same lineup that Bernadine Skillern saw—but Hubbard did not identify anyone in the lineup as the gunman.

Leodis Wilkerson was a twelve-year-old child who was on the parking lot and witnessed the murder. Wilkerson was interviewed by the police at the time. Wilkerson has recently stated that he distinctly remembers that the gunman was shorter than the victim. Bobby Lambert was five feet six inches. Stephen's wife Lorna riding in the front seat, described the man as shorter than her husband who was 5'7". The Stephens were not interviewed by the police at the time. They contacted Gary's attorney in April 1993 after hearing the case.

Gary's court-appointed lawyer did not present at trial four individuals who had been with Gary the night the murder took place. Loraine Johnson, William Chambers, Mary Brown, and Dorothy Shields all remember Gary being present in the yard area of the Hoffman housing complex on the night of the murder.

Loraine Johnson is Gary's cousin. At the time she lived in one of the four houses numbered one through four at Hoffman. There is an open area adjacent to the fourplex where people often meet and pass time. She remembers the night of May 13, for several reasons. Her grandmother's birthday had just occurred on May 11 and her cousin's birthday was on May 15. That evening the group discussed celebrating her cousin's birthday. Loraine swore in an affidavit that Gary arrived before 6 P.M. and stayed with the group until around 1 A.M. the following morning, except for one period of time. At one point in the evening, before dark, Gary and their cousin William Chambers walked to a nearby store and bought beverages. Loraine said they were only gone for about fifteen minutes and was positive that the errand took place prior to 9 P.M.

Another of Gary's cousins, William Henry Chambers, was also present. He lived at Hoffman with his grandmother. In a sworn affidavit, Chambers stated that Gary arrived before 5 P.M. and stayed until around 1:30 A.M. when his grandmother called him into the house. Chambers was certain of the date because the group had discussed plans for celebrating his birthday two days later.

Chambers was with Gary the entire evening and accompanied Gary on their trip to the neighborhood store to buy drinks. He said Gary could not have killed the man they say he did, that it was just not possible.

Mary Brown, a friend, and Dorothy Shields, a neighbor who lived in the fourplex, were also present the entire evening. The four witnesses who were with Gary were never contacted by his court-appointed lawyer nor the investigator. In her affidavit, Loraine Johnson said that she went to the trial and talked with Gary's attorney. She stated that upon learning that Gary had been found guilty, she was shocked that the attorney had not called her or the other three witnesses to testify.

After Gary was convicted, the jury was asked to determine punishment. The court instructed the jury to answer three questions: whether the crime was deliberate; whether the convicted individual would represent a future danger; and whether the killing was unreasonable in response to a provocation, if any, by the deceased. When the sentencing jury answered all questions yes, the death penalty was automatically imposed.

Gary was seventeen at the time of the murder and eighteen at the time of his trial. The jury that convicted Gary on the unreliable eyewitness testimony of one person sentenced him to death without hearing any information about his childhood of poverty and abuse.

The courts have been closely divided about the constitutionality of Gary's death sentence. On March 7, 1982, a three-judge panel of the Fifth Circuit Court of Appeals held that Gary's sentence violated the Constitution because his jury was unable to consider fully his youth in deciding whether he should be sentenced to death instead of life.

That decision was later overturned by the entire Fifth Circuit Court of Appeals in a seven-to-six decision. The six dissenting judges believed that Gary's sentencing procedure was unconstitutional and that his death sentence should have been vacated. On appeal, the U.S. Supreme Court, in a five-to-four decision, refused to consider the merits of his constitutional arguments and upheld his death sentence.

The Supreme Court agreed to reach the merits of Gary's constitutional arguments in another case involving the death sentence of an African-American youth who was nineteen at the time of the offense. This case, *Dorsey Johnson* v. *Texas,* was argued to the Court on April 26, 1993. A decision is expected to be issued soon. If these arguments prevail before the Supreme Court, it will mean that Gary's death sentence violates the United States Constitution. It is by these narrowest of margins that Gary Graham stands at death's door today.

Gary is now twenty-nine years old. He has grown up on

death row. During this time, Gary has taken impressive measures to improve himself. Although he has always maintained he is innocent of the murder of Bobby Lambert, he is open about the fact that as a teenager he was involved in criminal activity.

In prison, Gary has shown a remarkable commitment to change his life and contribute to the well-being of others. Gary is one of the founders of a death row newspaper. The *Endeavor* seeks to publish the writings of death row inmates and their families and to educate the public about the death penalty. Gary is enrolled in a paralegal course through the Blackstone School of Law and has assisted other prisoners with their cases.

As people have learned about Gary's case, they have gotten involved in it. Public outrage that the State of Texas could execute an innocent man has prompted calls for action from individuals and organizations across Texas, America, and the world.

Former New Mexico Governor Toney Anaya, Harry Belafonte, former First Lady Rosalynn Carter, former Ohio Governor Richard Celeste, Ossie Davis, Ruby Dee, Danny Glover, Congressman Henry B. Gonzalez, Kerry Kennedy Cuomo, Rev. Jesse Jackson, Coretta Scott King, Dr. Joseph Lowery, Lionel Ritchie, Kenny Rogers, and Bishop Desmond Tutu are among the people who have taken the time to get involved on Gary's behalf.

Gary was scheduled to be executed on April 29, but because of questions raised in this case that deserve further examination Governor Ann Richards granted a thirty-day reprieve only hours before the execution was to take place. Gary's attorneys have requested a hearing before the Texas Board of Pardons and Paroles to consider the overwhelming weight of evidence that Gary in innocent.

Just this year in a landmark case, *Herrera* v. *Texas,* the U.S. Supreme Court ruled that executive clemency was the traditional remedy to examine claims of innocence not presented at trial and unable to be examined by courts due to states' laws governing court procedures. The Court called the clemency process the fail-safe in the criminal justice system, designed to address flaws that the courts could not correct.

Courts have acted to correct several recent injustices in Texas. Clarence Brandley and Randall Dale Adams both served years on death row, their cries of innocence unheard until the news media examined their cases. Both have been released from Texas prisons. In another infamous Texas case, Lenell Geter was sentenced to life in prison after being identified by five eyewitnesses. As CBS News' "60 Minutes" revealed, Geter was innocent—wrongly accused, mistakenly identified, and unjustly convicted.

The Board of Pardons and Paroles, which would have to recommend clemency to the governor before any action could be taken, has thus far refused to consider Gary's case. Prominent Texas attorneys have written the governor and the board, urging that a meaningful, identifiable clemency review process be established. In the nearly twenty years since the reintroduction of the death penalty to Texas, the board has only held one clemency hearing in a capital case, and it has not reviewed a capital case with a claim of actual innocence.

Following the governor's reprieve, a June 3 execution date was set for Gary. On June 2, the nine judges of the Texas Court of Criminal Appeals granted Gary a stay pending the U.S. Supreme Court's ruling in the Johnson case. Gary and his supporters continue to press his claim of innocence.

14

A Death Row Inmate
Speaks to Youth

Ricky Smith

I've been on Tennessee's death row for about ten years. I don't want to scare kids out there, but perhaps something I say will reach some of you. I come to Tennessee's death row when I was about twenty-two years old and I've been here for the past ten years. I've seen a lot of things since I've been here.

You see when I grew up, I grew up where I didn't have no role models. So the things I looked up to was the things I thought was the way of life for me at that particular time. I grew up running around the street corners and hanging around with different people. The things that I did, I did because of peer pressure. I looked at people and they told me it was cool to do this, and cool to do that. In other words I listened to them instead of listening to my parents.

A lot of us grow up looking for things to be the way we want them to be instead of the way things are supposed to be in life. I remember a story called the *Wizard of Oz*. When Dorothy left home, she was looking for a place better than what was at home. She went out in the world and found a lot of wicked

189

things, same way I went out. I went out in the world, and instead of listening to my parents, I started listening to those who told me what was wrong. Because I wanted to hear something besides "no," I wanted to hear "yes, I can do that," when all the time they were leading me astray. They were leading me down the wrong paths.

I got out there and got hooked up in drugs, got hooked into doing a lot of crimes, and being with people I shouldn't have been with. I guess you could say this came about because I didn't have no respect for myself, I didn't have no respect for my parents. When I was home, they were always telling me that I got to mow the yard, or to do some cleaning around the house. See, to me that was something I thought I didn't have to do, and it was something I didn't understand. At the time they were teaching me responsibility and respect.

No sooner had my mother left out of the driveway when I called my friends over and they'd pick me up. I had made a decision that my friends were more important to me than my parents were. The things my friends wanted me to do were more important to me than the things my parents wanted me to do. Because I didn't do what my parents wanted me to do, I did what my friends did. Because of that, I'm sitting here on Tennessee's death row.

I know some kids out there think you're living a pretty good life, a tough life. The things you do, ain't nobody there to stop you . . . but you're wrong. See, because now, here I am ten years later and I don't have the freedom to go and mow that yard like I wish I had, or to wash the dishes or clean the house that I could have done back then. I don't even have the freedom to see my nieces and nephews grow up, and I've got a lot of them.

They come see me once a month. You might think when you get locked up you don't lose. You lose a lot of things . . .

you lose your family, you lose your life, you lose your self-respect. You can't be proud of sitting on death row. You can't be proud of sitting in prison. And if you do, that's the sign of a fool. And I don't think any of you out there are fools—I think you have the wrong people out there telling you the wrong advice. Telling the wrong things. Things you think you need to know to be around them. Eventually, you're going to end up in a place like I am. And then you'll look back and see, those friends, they weren't your friends at all.

They were people leading you down the same path they were leading themselves down. See, because just like we have responsibilities, they have responsibilities too. Just like your parents told you something to do, nine times out of ten, their parents told them what to do. They wasn't doing it, so you see you're in the same boat.

I'm just telling you like it is. Hopefully, something I tell you will get through to you. Your parents love you. If they didn't they wouldn't be doing the things they do to keep you out of trouble, to keep you in school, to try to show you right from wrong, to be proud of you. Somewhere down the line you're going to wish you had those morals they tried to teach you about. Somewhere down the line, you're going to wish you went to your parents and talked to them, instead of talking to your friends. 'Cause your friends don't mean you no good. Don't sit back and let peer pressure talk you into doing something you don't want to do. If you don't want to do something, say you don't want to do it. Stand up for it—don't go along with it just because that's what the crowd is doing. You don't have to be a part of the crowd. You can stand up and be for real all on your own. You can make your life count for something, 'cause a lot of us wish we had that opportunity to do it again. But we don't know if we can . . . or not. One thing we can say

is, the place we're at is real. It's not a dream, it's not a nightmare, it's a real place. Believe it or not, it makes you come to
your reality real soon. It makes you aware of what you have and
don't have. It makes you aware of what life is really all about.
And if you don't know what life is all about, you're lost. You're
alone. And that's a lonely place to be.

15

"Isolation That You Can't Understand" The Ron Harries Story

Shirley Dicks

Ron Harries was born on December 30, 1950, into a poverty-stricken family. His mother, Katherine, was seventeen years old and his father was in prison during most of her pregnancy. She finally moved to the city to live with her parents, where she had to pay room and board. It wasn't long before Katherine was pregnant again. Then she moved to the Valley View Project and lived on welfare. Although she tried very hard to keep her family clean and fed, it wasn't easy.

Katherine's husband, Bill, came home from prison, but life with him was not what she had expected. He began to beat her in front of Ron, who was only six years old at the time. Fortunately, Bill was never home very much, but it was always long enough to get Katherine pregnant again. Soon he was back in prison as she gave birth to two more children.

Ron never enjoyed the security of a stable home life. His father, uncles, and most of his male role models were in and out of prison all of Ron's life. His grandmother and mother fought over Ron and he was placed first with one, then the other. His grandmother enrolled him in a Catholic school, where he was teased unmercifully by the other children. He often had to fight his way out of scrapes. His grandmother would then tie him to the bed and make him recite the rosary. He was told he was a bad kid over and over again.

Because he was passed around from place to place, Ron did not enjoy security. He saw himself as a bad boy who no one wanted and stayed high on drugs or alcohol.

Ron first got into trouble at the age of nine and was placed in a boys' home. After that, he was in court more and more. In the beginning, his mother would come and get him, but then she would not come get him or would not show up in court when he got into trouble.

After that, Ron lived in a string of boys' homes and halfway houses. He would run away regularly to avoid the beatings, fighting, rapes, and murders that he was constantly seeing at home and in the institutions. He spent two-thirds of his young life in institutions and they were a way of life to him.

On August 13, 1963, he was sent to the Starr Commonwealth for Boys. It offered boys a home environment through its cottage-styled living. Twelve boys and two house parents lived in each family. Each cottage family organized meals and activities. Ron began to like living there. He remembered loving his house parents as he had never loved anyone before. He said the two years at Starr Commonwealth were the best years of his life. He remembers only one visit from his mother in all that time. She had remarried. Her husband, Blain, was good to Ron, but only as long as he was sober, and Blain was usually drunk.

At fourteen Ron ended up on the Hudson Farm—a place where only those who had been in several lesser security institutions were sent. Most of the boys at the farm were older and they taught Ron well. They fought with chains and pipes, taught him how to use drugs and break into places. Rapes were frequent.

When he was sixteen and in a boys' industrial school, Ron saw his best friend murdered right in front of his eyes. After that, he just didn't care anymore and became solely interested in survival.

Ron had lived a lifetime in his early years, knowing little love or family living. At eighteen he joined the U.S. Marines, going to boot camp in 1968. While in the Marines he received clerical training and got his GED. Ron had a good job in the PX. Unfortunately, he no sooner left this controlled environment than he was in trouble again. He went to see his grandmother who said he was evil and just a bum. He returned to his mother and she took him in.

Ron married Sue in 1971, and they had a daughter. He tried to go straight. He got a job, bought new furniture, and made a down payment on a suburban house. After they moved in, Ron became jealous and possessive and would not let Sue leave the house without him. Ron's downhill slide began when his father was released from prison. Ron wanted to impress him, so together they drank and ran scams. Before long Ron came home and found the house empty. Sue had left him with nothing.

Ron started to look for his wife and child, but it was only after he beat up his father that he learned where they had gone. Ron went to Ohio to find them, high on drugs, committing robbery after robbery to pay for his search. He took a hostage in a robbery attempt, but after holding her for a couple of hours, he let her go unharmed. The police picked him up, and he was charged with armed robbery, kidnapping, and possession of a firearm while committing a felony. He received a sentence of six to twenty years.

Ron spent six years in prison. He was transferred to the

prison in Lucasville, Ohio. This state prison held all the high-security-risk prisoners. Ron did his time. When he was finally released, he was still kept captive by a drug habit and an institutionalized mind.

Ron and his friend headed for Tennessee. They planned to pull three or four robberies and then travel on to Florida. On January 22, 1981, Ron went into a Jiffy Market in Kingsport, Tennessee. He needed money for his drug habit. "I was high on drugs at the time. All I wanted was a little money and I won't lie about that. During the course of the robbery the clerk's boyfriend tried to thwart it. He screamed at me and ran at me. The gun was pointed at her and it went off." Rhonda Greene fell dead in front of him. Her cousin came over and Ron made her give him the cash. He could have killed her too, but left without harming her. For this crime, he was given the death sentence.

In June 1984, Ron gave up his appeals. He maintains that he is ready to die to shock the public into seeing the gruesome reality of the death sentence. Having to stay in a solitary cell, cut off from normal communication from others, is a depressing experience that not many people can cope with. Death row residents are hated and feared by others, and their lives have no meaning. "I've made my peace with God, but it took a long time," he said. Federal Judge John Nixon canceled Ron's execution pending a hearing on whether drugs that had been given to him impaired his reasoning.

Harries's mother and four brothers had just completed their final visit with him. They were going to return to Cleveland, Ohio, to await news of his scheduled execution.

"My mother sat here crying on her last visit," Ron said. "She was crying not only for me, but for Rhonda Greene." He doesn't expect Rhonda's family will ever forgive him, but he asks that they at least give him the opportunity to tell them he's sorry. "If killing my son would bring back Rhonda, I would find some meaning in Ron's death and I would accept that," Ron's mother said, but she was unable to understand a revenge killing.

"I made the ultimate mistake, but don't use the Bible with an eye for an eye, just say you're mad, you hate me for what I've done to your family, but don't say its God's will." Ron said. "I killed somebody and there's no way that I can make amends for that and there is no way that I can condone it or make excuses for it, but I didn't torture Rhonda Greene. I know I was guilty, but it was not intentional or premeditated." In one conversation Ron told a friend that he had never had a single happy day in his life. He wonders why he shot Rhonda when other armed robberies ended with no one hurt. He cannot escape the memories that haunt him at night. His own daughter bears the same name as the girl he killed.

Governor Alexander refused to commute Harries's death sentence. Letters poured in from all over the world asking that Harries not be executed. One such letter said, "Stop executions in Tennessee, in the USA and all over the world. Reprieve Ronald Harries that you yourself get not involved in murder. The fact that the death penalty is abolished in the Federal Republic of Germany by the fundamental law says that the death penalty is unworthy of a nation like the United States. In our meaning, the death penalty is deeply cruel and violates the dignity of human beings."

Judge Nixon stayed the execution days before it was scheduled. A next-friend suit was filed by friends of Ron who feel that he was not of sane mind when he gave up his appeals. Attorneys said conditions on death row make Ron unable to make rational decisions.

Ron spoke of the conditions on death row.

It's filthy and dirty in our cells. Our showers are cut at eight minutes. We have to wear hot, unsanitary orange jumpsuits all the time. When prisoners ask for toilet paper, they are asked by guards if they think this is the Holiday Inn. I had ear surgery and my ear started bleeding. I didn't have medical attention for more than twenty-six hours.

Death row is isolation that you can't understand unless you live it. Every day is the same. You come out for a shower and if the weather is nice enough, you get to go outside for one hour. The exercise yard is small cages that have wire mesh even on the top so the sun cannot shine. All I have to offer is to write down things I feel because I hope somebody will say this will keep someone from doing the same thing I did. I lay back and wonder how I'll act when it comes down. Will I scream and holler on my way over there or will I be manly? I go to bed at night and hear the noises around me. Some radios playing, some televisions, and some sniffing. Then I wonder if I'll be in here a year or will I be dead.

When asked if he was ready to die, Ron said,

It's not so much being ready. I've accepted it. I think God has forgiven me for what happened. My relatives are upset, they cry when they talk to me. They want me to change my mind and resume my appeals. The state has had control over my life all the years I was locked up. I don't want them to have control over my death.

I'm trying to make it harder for other death row inmates to be electrocuted. The point is the inhumanness of the death penalty has to be brought out. That's good. That's positive.

Judge Nixon ruled that Ron was incompetent to decide his fate. Nixon based his ruling on testimony of psychiatrists who after examining Ron said he was not competent to make a decision while living in the inhumane conditions on death row. Nixon also ruled that the next friend petitioners who intervened on Harries behalf when he dropped his appeals have standing and can appeal the inmate's conviction. The stay of execution will remain in effect until disposition of the petitioners' lawsuit against the state in which they challenge the constitutionality of the death penalty, with or without Harries.

I want to tell you kids out there that there are people out there who will help you, who want to help you. I'm forty-three years old now, and have been in an institution for over thirty years of that forty-three. I've done everything from heroin to crack to coke; anything you name, I've done it. I've been in gangs, just on and on. By my sitting here telling you what it's like, you might not listen. I have brothers that I've never met, I've got a granddaughter I've never seen. I lost my mother five months ago.

What I'm telling you is if you don't straighten your life out, go to someone and talk to them. This isn't any place to live. I've come close to being executed. Since that time, I've realized that as long as there's life there's hope.

Some of you kids out there who are hanging around the corner or whatever. You're not tough. I've been through the whole scheme, I thought I was a tough guy, I fronted for people, I've done all sorts of things even though I knew they were wrong, just because I wanted to belong. You don't need to belong. What you need is an education. If you have a problem, talk to somebody. Otherwise you're going to be sitting here like me and it's a power game. It's a bingo game and one of these days my number is going to come up, and in my opinion it won't be long.

When you walk into a store to steal something, then it

progresses to holding somebody, pretty soon it will progress to where you kill somebody, then the state is going to take your life. Try to straighten your act up.

You can look at me and say he's trying to give me a line or something. I don't give a damn what you do or how you do it. I'm telling you if you don't straighten your act up, if you act a fool—and some of you are acting the fool thinking you can get away from it—but eventually you're going to wind up in a six-by-eight cell, missing your family, and you're going to die before you see them again.

16

An Ex-Biker Rehabilitated on Death Row

Gerald Laney

I'm what you'd call a three-time loser. I used to be like a Pepsi can: I was from the new generation, strong and fresh, I thought I was the real thing. I let my so-called friends use me, and they used me. When I got put in jail I was crushed, 'cause they didn't want anything to do with me anymore 'cause I didn't have anything they wanted. But I've been recycled. I don't let my friends use me anymore, and if you were smart, you'd be the same way.

I'm just one in about 104 death-row inmates scheduled to die. But what does matter to me is you kids out there and your future. The choices you make right now in your life will not only affect you but your whole family. So you'd better make the right choices, 'cause I can tell you when you make the wrong choices, what you go through, how much it hurts, and most of all . . . what you do to your family and loved ones.

For the last twenty years of my life, I've been in prisons, and I've spent the past thirteen years on Tennessee's death row. At one time I slept about twenty feet from the electric chair, called "Old Sparky." There wasn't a day that went by that I didn't think about death and dying in that electric chair and I thought about what got me there. It was not going to school, not getting a good education, using drugs and alcohol, being a gang member, and choosing the wrong kind of friends.

I went to a man's home. He had bought ten pounds of marijuana from members of our motorcycle club. He paid half and missed a couple of deadlines, and they sent me there to talk to him. When he got out of his car, I seen how big he was. He had a bag in one hand, a gun in the other. When he saw me, he threw the bag and fired. I remember seeing the flash of that gun and the burn in my side. I knew he had shot me, and like a chain reaction, I returned fire. When the smoke cleared, I was lying on his carport. I had been shot four times, lying in a pool of blood. Choker had been shot down and was killed.

Right when I was on the brink of death God came to me in a vision and showed me how wrong I'd lived my life. He give me back my life that night and none of the doctors could believe it. When I came out of my coma the doctors told me I was lucky to be alive. But you know I didn't feel too lucky.

I was sent to death row and it was dirty, with roaches crawling up the walls. I saw how nasty that little cell was. The next morning they brought me my food and slid it under the door of my cell like I was some kind of animal. That evening they asked me if I wanted to go to the exercise yard and I told them yes. They put my hands behind my back and let me out to the exercise yard. I looked around and it looked like I was in a dog kennel. I was out there for one hour, ten minutes to shower, and the rest of the time I was locked up in my cell.

That's when I found out that three walk was nicknamed the dungeon. I didn't know if it was cold or hot, raining or sun shining. I never saw the stars or the moon. See, we never had a window in my cell and for ten years I had to live like that. It is the small things like walking on grass—I hadn't walked on grass in over thirteen years.

I met Frank Bambridge at that time. He stopped at my cell and I thought, "Here is another Jesus freak," 'cause God didn't have any meaning in my life. Our conversation was always limited. We became good friends.

I had become a big burden on my family and friends and I decided to kill myself. But that wasn't the answer. I put sheets up in the cell and was going to hang myself. I sat back on my bunk and wondered how in the world did I come to this place where I wanted to kill myself. I traced back in my mind to see if I could find the answers.

I remembered growing up in a small town in Clinchcove, Virginia. I come from a large family with five brothers and four sisters. And even though we didn't have as much as others, we had plenty of love for one another. I guess it was a struggle that we saw our parents going through to try and give us kids things, just to put food on the table, but they always gave us the love of God. And I remember going to school with my two older sisters and I was always bothered because they were smarter than me. But me, I just couldn't understand what my teacher was trying to teach me.

She thought I was lazy and didn't want to learn so she started to humiliate me in front of the others, like by drawing little circles on the blackboard and making me stand with my nose pressed against it, or having the class read out from the readers, and when it came my turn, she would get angry. She would run over and grab my hand and beat it with a ruler. I thought how embarrassing because all the other kids were laughing at me and things. And when we got to go outside I always had to stay in and get punished, but when I did go outside, I had to wear a hat that said I was a dunce. I couldn't read and I would sit on the steps of the school and cry my eyes out.

My sisters would feel sorry for me, but there wasn't anything they could do. So I just ended up hating school, hating my teachers, and ended up not trying to learn anything. When I got a little older, I found out I had a learning disability called dyslexia. That's when you see your alphabets upside down. I didn't know the difference between a B, D, E, P, M, W, or 9 and 6. I grew up not being able to read and write. And deep down I was ashamed of myself and I still am.

You think it's easy for me to tell you that I can't read and write? It's embarrassing, man. So I ended up hating school, hating my teacher, and ended up not learning anything. I remember it wasn't long after that my father tried to kill himself and I thank God that he didn't.

As I got a little older, I started hanging around this pool hall. I'd see these bikers come into the pool hall and they'd be wearing these motorcycle jackets and carrying guns. I seen how much respect they got from others. I saw a lot of drugs and money being made and I wanted to be a part of that. I knew I'd never be an A-1 student or make anything out of myself. But I thought if I got to be known as a tough guy, it was better than being known as a nobody.

So I started hanging around these bikers, and naturally I learned how to cuss, I learned how to steal, I learned how to sell drugs, and I learned how to do them. To put it plainly, I wasn't nothing but a foul mouth little punk. It wasn't long before I began taking these drugs to school to sell them. And the other kids thought I was cool and looked up to me as some kind of leader. But I wasn't being cool, I was being a fool. Because if I knew then what I know now, I'd have stayed in school, gotten an education, and made something of myself.

It wasn't long before I got kicked out of school and at the time I thought it was the happiest time of my life. So I just went back to the old motorcycle gang, wheeling, stealing, and doing drugs. I earned the nickname "Hustler" for my fast and easy way of earning money. But little did I know or care that the state of Tennessee had a cell waiting for me, and it was on Tennessee's death row.

It wasn't long before I got arrested and put in jail. My parents' darkest nightmare was coming true. I was on my way to prison. And when I saw that prison, it looked like an old castle I'd seen in story books. I stood in that breezeway, and I saw two men hugging and kissing. I thought to myself, oh God what have I gotten myself into, 'cause I never, ever forgot the sound of those steel doors closing behind me. 'Cause when I come off that prison, it was like stepping into a world of violence. I seen a lot of stealing, a lot of robbing, a lot of raping, and a lot of killings. I knew that sooner or later someone would try me and I would have to stand up for myself cause everyone knows that prison is the devil's playground where only the strong survive. It's a steel-and-concrete jungle where you learn how to kill or be killed.

You don't have much of a life in there. You don't even have a name, you have a number. You belong to the state and they tell you every move you make. They can treat you any way they want to and there's nothing you or anybody else can do about it.

Let me tell you how easy it is to die in prison. These two brothers had stolen a car and gone joyriding. They caught prison time and one day the youngest one was late for chow. He ran and got in front of others to be with his brother. A fight began and he was stabbed in the heart. He died in his brother's arms.

I could never tell you about all the violence I've seen in life, all the beatings, stabbings, and killings. The dreams I had when I was younger of being a tough guy was coming true. I became known as the National Enforcer for the motorcycle gangs. I loved it because prison had filled me with hate, and my lifestyle consisted of drugs, alcohol, and hatred and massive destruction. Even my fellow gang members feared Hustler because they knew there was nothing I wouldn't have done.

My dad used to tell me that I caused him more trouble than my brothers and sisters. But you know I didn't care how much I hurt my mother and dad and how much shame I put on our family. The only thing that was important was me being cool around all my friends.

So I know how you kids are under a lot of pressure. Some of you come from broken and abused homes and you think that's a good enough excuse to throw your lives away. I know when you're teenagers you think you're smart enough, and life is just a big bore, but I'm telling you from someone who can't read and write you're going to need all the education you can get. When you're out with your friends, your friends will put a lot of pressure on you, and talk you into doing a lot of stupid things like taking drugs and alcohol, 'cause I know that peer pressure is hell and you'd do anything to fit in with your friends.

But you'll get to the point where you're not using drugs and alcohol, it's the drugs and alcohol using you. 'Cause you'll start stealing from your friends and family. And if you're lucky, when you get caught, you'll just go to jail for a little while, but if you keep on robbing, stealing, and taking, you're going to prison, and you may end up losing your own life. Many of my friends have.

When I was young, I got my high school sweetheart pregnant. So we ran away, got married, and had a beautiful daughter. Shireen was her name. She's been the highlight of my life, just like you are to your parents. But see, I never was there for

Shireen, but she didn't use me for an excuse to throw her life away. She listened to me and went to school and stayed away from drugs and alcohol. Now, she's a sophomore in college and I am proud when she calls me her daddy.

A good education is the key to success. And it's not going out here trying to prove that you're tough, by doing drugs, joining gangs, robbing, stealing, and hurting people. 'Cause that just leads to a lonely and miserable life. I know 'cause that's the life I've led. And you think, "Man, why are you telling me this?" I'm doing this for each and every one of you. So you don't end up throwing your life away, like me and thousands like me. 'Cause I'm going to be handcuffed and taken to my cell where I'm going to have to spend my life if I'm not executed. Now that is real.

The last twenty years of my life have been a long and rough road to travel, but it was an easy one to find. My advice to you is stay out of jails 'cause they will take you away from everything you ever loved. Stay in school and get a good education and make something out of yourselves, and you won't end up blowing it like me.

17

Wrongly Convicted

Shirley Dicks

In 1972, when the Supreme Court ruled in *Furman* v *Georgia* that the death penalty as then applied was arbitrary and capricious and therefore unconstitutional, a majority of the justices expected that the adoption of narrowly crafted sentencing procedures would protect against innocent persons being sentenced to death. Yet the promise of *Furman* has not been fulfilled: innocent persons are still being sentenced to death, and the chances are high that innocent persons have been or will be executed. No issue posed by capital punishment is more disturbing to the public than the prospect that the government might execute an innocent person. A recent national poll found that the number one concern raising doubts among voters regarding the death penalty is the danger of a mistaken execution.

The Subcommittee on Civil and Constitutional Rights heard testimony from four men who were released from prison after serving years on death row, living proof that innocent people are sentenced to death. The hearing raised two questions: (1) just how frequently are innocent persons convicted and sentenced to death? and (2) what flaws in the system allow these injustices to occur? To answer these questions, Subcommittee Chairman Don Edwards called upon the Death Penalty Information Center to compile information on cases in the past twenty years where inmates had been released from death row after their innocence had been acknowledged. This report is based on the research of the center.

This report focuses on the past twenty years when convicted individuals have been released from death row because of new evidence that proved their innocence. The system of trials, appeals, and executive clemency fails to offer sufficient safeguards in protecting the innocent from being sentenced for execution. The role of current legal protection is addressed by looking at a few of the cases where death row inmates were later found to be innocent or were executed with their guilt still in doubt.

The most conclusive evidence that innocent people are condemned to death under modern death sentencing procedures comes from the surprisingly large number of people whose convictions have been overturned and who have been freed from death row. Four former death row inmates have been released from prison just this year after their innocence became apparent: Kirk Bloodsworth, Federico Macias, Walter McMillian, and Gregory Wilhoit.

Since 1973 significant evidence of their innocence has won at least forty-eight people release from prison after serving time on death row. In forty-three of these cases, the defendant was acquitted, pardoned, or charges were dropped. In three of the cases, a compromise was reached and the defendants were immediately released upon pleading to a lesser offense.

The forty-eight cases illustrate the flaws inherent in the death-sentencing systems used in the states. Some of these men were convicted because the court heard perjured testimony or because the prosecutor improperly withheld exculpatory evidence. In other cases, racial prejudice was a determining factor. In others, defense counsel failed to conduct the necessary investigation that would have disclosed exculpatory information.

Racial Prejudice: Clarence Brandley

Sometimes racial prejudice propels an innocent person into the role of despicable convict. In 1980, a sixteen-year-old white girl named Cheryl Dee Ferguson was raped and murdered at the Texas high school. Suspicion turned to the school's five janitors. One of the janitors later testified that the police looked at Clarence Brandley, the only black in the group. and said, "Since you're the nigger, you're elected."

Brandley was convicted and sentenced to death by an all-white jury after two trials. The prosecutor used his peremptory strikes to eliminate all blacks in the jury pool. Eleven months after the conviction, Brandley's attorneys learned that 166 of the 309 exhibits used at the trial, many of which offered grounds for appeal, had vanished.

After six years of fruitless appeals and civil rights demonstrations in support of Brandley, the Texas Court of Criminal Appeals ordered an evidentiary hearing to investigate all the allegations that had come to light. The presiding judge wrote a stinging condemnation of the procedures used in Brandley's case and stated that, "The court unequivocally concludes that the color of Clarence Brandley's skin was a substantial factor which pervaded all aspects of the State's capital prosecution of him." Brandley was eventually released in 1990, and all charges were dismissed.

It took many years and a tremendous effort by outside counsel, civil rights organizers, special investigators, and the media to save Brandley's life. Others on death row find it nearly impossible to get even a hearing on a claim of innocence.

The Pressure to Prosecute: Walter McMillian

"I was wrenched from my family, from my children, from my grandchildren, and from my friends, from my work that I loved, and was placed in an isolation cell, the size of a shoe box, with no sunlight, no companionship, and no work for nearly six years. Every minute of every day, I knew I was innocent."

In 1986, in the small town of Monroeville, Alabama, an eighteen-year-old white woman was shot to death in the dry cleaners around 10 A.M. Although the murder shocked the town, the police arrested no one for eight months. Johnny McMillian was a black man who lived in the next town. He had been dating a white woman and his son had married a white woman, neither of which made McMillian popular in Monroeville.

On the day of the murder, McMillian was at a fish fry with his friends and relatives. Many of the people at the fish fry gave testimony at the trial that McMillian could not have committed the murder of Rhonda Morrison because he was with them all day. Nevertheless, he was arrested, tried, and convicted of the murder. Indeed, McMillian was placed on death row upon his arrest, well before his trial. No physical evidence linked him to the crime, but three people testifying at his trial connected him with the murder. All three witnesses received favors from the state for their incriminating testimony. All three later recanted their testimony, including the only eyewitness, who stated that he was pressured by the prosecutors to implicate McMillian in the crime. The jury in the trial recommended a life sentence for McMillian, but the judge overruled this recommendation and sentenced him to death. McMillian's case went through four rounds of appeal, all of which were denied. New attorneys not paid by the state of Alabama voluntarily took over the case and eventually found that the prosecutors had illegally withheld evidence that would have pointed to McMillian's innocence. A story about the case appeared on CBS-TV's "60 Minutes" on November 22, 1992. Finally, the state agreed to investigate its earlier handling of the case and then admitted that a grave mistake had been made. Mr. McMillian was freed into the welcoming arms of his family and friends on March 3, 1993.

Inadequate Counsel: Federico Macias

Federico Macias's court-appointed lawyer did virtually nothing to prepare Macias's case for trial. Marcias was sentenced to death in Texas in 1984. Two days before his scheduled execution, Macias received a stay. New counsel from the large Skadden, Arps law firm had entered the case and devoted to it the firm's considerable resources and expertise. Mr. Macias's conviction was overturned via a federal writ of habeas corpus, which was upheld by a unanimous panel of the U.S. Court of Appeals for the Fifth Circuit in December 1992. The court found that Macias's original counsel not only was grossly ineffective, but also had missed considerable evidence pointing to Macias's innocence. The court concluded: "We are left with the firm conviction that Macias was denied his constitutional right to adequate counsel in a capital case in which actual innocence was a close question." The state paid defense counsel the sum of $11.84 per hour, and unfortunately, the justice system got only what it paid for. Macias was freed when the grand jury, which now had access to the evidence developed by the Skadden, Arps attorneys, refused to re-indict him.

Many similar stories can be told of defendants who have spent years on death row, some coming within hours of their executions, only to be released by the court with all charges dropped. What is noteworthy about the cases outlined above is that they are recent examples that illustrate that mistaken death sentences are not a relic of the past.

Official Misconduct

While Clarence Chance and Benny Powell were not sentenced to death, their convictions for murder illustrate the dangers of overzealous police work. They were released from prison after Jim McCloskey of Centurion Ministries took on their case and demonstrated their innocence. The city of Los Angeles awarded them $7 million and the judge termed the police department's conduct reprehensible, while apologizing for the gross injustices that occurred.

In some cases these released men were found innocent as a result of sheer luck. Walter McMillian's volunteer outside counsel had obtained from the prosecutors an audiotape of one of the key witnesses' statements incriminating Mr. McMillian. After listening to the statement, the attorney flipped the tape over to see if anything was on the other side. It was only then that he heard the same witness complaining that he was being pressured to frame Mr. McMillian. With that fortuitous break, the whole case against McMillian began to fall apart.

Similarly, proving the innocence of Kirk Bloodsworth was more a matter of chance than the orderly working of the appeals process. Only a scientific breakthrough, and an appellate lawyer's initiative in trying it after years of failed appeals, allowed Bloodsworth to prove his innocence. Even then, the prosecutor was not bound under Maryland law to admit this new evidence. Furthermore, not every death row inmate is afforded, after conviction, the quality of counsel and resources that Walter McMillian and Federico Macias were fortunate to have during their postconviction proceedings. Many of those on death row go for years without any attorney at all.

Most of the releases from death row over the past twenty years came only after many years and many failed appeals. The average length of time between conviction and release was almost seven years for the forty-eight death row inmates released since 1970.

Too often, the reviews afforded death row inmates on appeal and habeas corpus simply do not offer a meaningful opportunity to present claims of innocence. Many states simply have no formal procedure for hearing new evidence of a defendant's innocence prior to his execution date. After trial, the legal system becomes locked in a battle over procedural issues rather than a reexamination of guilt or innocence. The all-night struggle to stay the execution of Leonel Herrera in 1992, even after the U.S. Supreme Court had agreed to hear his constitutional challenge, is an example of how much pressure is exerted to proceed with executions.

Accounts that report that a particular case has been appealed numerous times before many judges may be misleading. Most often, procedural issues, rather than the defendant's innocence are being argued and reviewed in these appeals. For example, when Roger Keith Coleman was executed in Virginia last year, it was reported that his last appeal to the Supreme Court was Coleman's sixteenth round in court. However, the Supreme Court had earlier declared that Coleman's constitutional claims were barred from any review in federal court because his previous attorneys had filed an appeal too late in 1986. His evidence was similarly excluded from review in state court as well. Instead, Coleman's innocence was debated only in the news media, and considerable doubt concerning his guilt accompanied him to his execution.

Role of the Media: Randall Dale Adams

One unpredictable element affecting the release of an innocent person is the involvement of the media. In Randall Dale Adams case, film producer Errol Morris went to Texas to make a documentary on Dr. James Grigson, the notorious "Dr. Death." Grigson would claim 100 percent certainty for his courtroom predictions that a particular defendant would kill again, and he made such a prediction about Randall Adams.

In the course of his investigation of Grigson, Morris became interested in Adams's plight and helped unearth layers of misconduct by the prosecutor in that case. He also obtained on tape a virtual confession by another person. Morris's movie *The Thin Blue Line* told Randall Adams's story in a way no one had seen before. The movie was released in 1988, and Adams was freed the following year.

The trial is obviously the critical time for the defendant to make his or her case for innocence. Unfortunately, the manner in which defense counsel are selected and compensated for death penalty trials does not always protect the defendant's rights at this pivotal time. Most defendants facing the death penalty cannot afford to hire their own attorney, so the state is required to provide them with one. Some states have public defenders' offices staffed by attorneys trained to handle such cases. In other states, attorneys are appointed from the local community, and the quality of representation is spotty.

Federico Macias is certainly not alone with respect to ineffective counsel. Stories regarding deficient representation in death penalty cases are rampant. The subcommittee has held several hearings documenting this problem. Although death penalty law is a highly specialized and complex form of litigation, there is no guarantee that the attorney appointed to this critical role will have the necessary expertise to handle it. There is no independent appointing authority to select only qualified counsel for these cases, and attorneys are frequently underpaid and understaffed, with few resources for this critical undertaking.

Before trial, the arrested defendant need do nothing to prove his innocence. The burden is completely on the prosecution to prove charges beyond a reasonable doubt that the individual is guilty of the crimes. However, after someone is found guilty, the presumption shifts in favor of the state. The burden is now on the defendant to prove to a court that something went wrong in arriving at the determination of guilt. It is no longer enough to raise a reasonable doubt. To overturn a conviction, the evidence must be compelling, and violations of constitutional rights by the state will be forgiven as long as they are judged to have been harmless.

If an innocent defendant is convicted, he generally has little time to collect and present new evidence that might reverse his conviction. In Texas, for example, a defendant has only thirty days after his conviction to present new evidence. The state strictly adheres to that rule. Sixteen other states require that a new trial motion based on new evidence be filed within sixty days of judgment. Thus, even a compelling claim of innocence, such as a videotape of someone else committing the crime, as recently hypothesized by Justice Anthony Kennedy in oral arguments of *Herrera,* does not guarantee a review in state or federal court.

All death row inmates are assured representation to make one direct appeal in their state courts. If that appeal is denied, representation is no longer assured. In states like Texas and California with large death row populations, many defendants sentenced to death are not currently being represented by any attorney. Obviously, such a defendant's opportunity to uncover evidence to prove his innocence is greatly reduced, even assuming a court would hear the evidence if it was found.

When someone has been unjustly convicted under circumstances similar to those described above, he can challenge that conviction in federal court through the writ of habeas corpus. Although numerous legislative proposals to limit habeas corpus have failed in the past few years, the opportunity for using this writ has already been stringently narrowed by recent Supreme Court decisions.

The Supreme Court has denied habeas review of claims from prisoners on death row with persuasive, newly discovered evidence of their innocence. Leonel Herrera presented affidavits and positive polygraph results from a variety of witnesses, including an eyewitness to the murder and a former Texas state judge, both of whom stated that someone else had committed the crime. However, the Supreme Court ruled that Herrera was not entitled to a federal hearing on this evidence and was told that his only recourse was the clemency process of the state of Texas. Herrera was subsequently executed.

Death row inmates who claim their innocence are therefore often forced to rely on procedural claims, but those too are being foreclosed by the Supreme Court. For example, Gary Graham's case has gained national attention because he has made a substantial claim of innocence. However, the barriers to getting such new evidence before the courts have necessitated that the defense pursue other claims that only affect his sentence. Death penalty attorneys realize that proving their clients innocent after execution is of no value to the dead.

But when Gary Graham claimed that the Texas death penalty procedures did not allow consideration of his youth at the time of the crime, the U.S. Supreme Court refused to even consider the question. The Court said that even if he was right in his claim, ruling in his favor would create a new rule of law and no such rule could apply retroactively to his case.

Another recent narrowing of the writ requires federal courts to reject all claims if the proper procedures were not followed by the defendant in state court. Roger Coleman, for example, filed his Virginia state appeal three days late and this error by his attorneys barred any consideration of his federal constitutional claims. Coleman was executed without a federal court hearing his claim. Similarly, if a claim is not raised on a defendant's first habeas petition, the claim—with rare exceptions—is automatically rejected, even if the government withheld the very evidence the defendant would have needed to raise the claim in his first petition.

For the innocent defendant, the last avenue of relief is clemency from the executive branch. All death penalty states have some form of pardon power vested either in the governor or in a board of review. However, clemencies in death penalty cases are extremely rare. Since the death penalty was reinstated in 1976, forty-eight hundred death sentences have been imposed but fewer than three dozen clemencies have been granted on defendants' petitions. In Texas, the state with the greatest number of executions, no clemencies have been granted.

The procedures for clemency are as varied as the states. In many states the governor has the final say on granting a commutation of a death sentence. Since the governor is an elected official and since there is virtually no review of his or her decision, there is the danger that political motivations can influence the decisions. Many of the commutations that have been granted in the past twenty years were granted by governors only as they were leaving office.

Other arrangements are also subject to political pressures. In Texas, a board must first recommend clemency to the governor. However, the board is appointed by the governor and is not required to meet or hear testimony to review a case. Recently, a judge in Texas held that this lack of process violated Gary Graham's constitutional rights and ordered a hearing to review his claims of innocence.

In Nebraska, Nevada, and Florida, the chief state prosecutor sits on the clemency review board. Generally, there are no procedural guarantees to assure that a claim of innocence that has been barred review by the courts will be fully aired for clemency. As Justice Blackmun recently pointed out: "Whatever procedures a State might adopt to hear actual innocent claims, one thing is certain; the possibility of executive clemency is not sufficient to satisfy the requirements of the Eighth and Fourteenth Amendments."

Thus the prospect of clemency provides only the thinnest thread of hope and is certainly no guarantee against the execution of an innocent individual.

It is an inescapable fact of our criminal justice system that innocent people are too often convicted of crimes. Sometimes only many years later, in the course of a defendant's appeals, or as a result of extralegal developments, new evidence will emerge that clearly demonstrates that the wrong person was prosecuted and convicted of a crime.

Americans are justifiably concerned about the possibility

that an innocent person may be executed. Capital punishment in the United States today provides no reliable safeguards against this danger. Errors can and have been made repeatedly in the trial of death penalty cases because of poor representation, racial prejudice, prosecutorial misconduct, or simply the presentation of erroneous evidence. Once convicted, a death row inmate faces serious obstacles in convincing any tribunal that he is innocent.

The cases discussed in this report are the ones in which innocence was uncovered before execution. Once an execution occurs, the small group of lawyers who handle postconviction proceedings in death penalty cases in the United States move on to the next crisis. Investigations of innocence end after execution. If an innocent person was among the 222 people executed in the United States since Furman, nobody in the legal system is paying attention any longer.

Many death penalty convictions and sentences are overturned on appeal, but too frequently the discovery of error is the result of finding expert appellate counsel, a sympathetic judge willing to waive procedural barriers, and a compelling set of facts that can overcome the presumption of guilt. Not all convicted death row inmates are likely to have these opportunities.

Judging by past experience, a substantial number of death row inmates are indeed innocent, and there is a high risk that some of them will be executed. The danger is inherent in the punishment itself and the fallibility of human nature. The danger is enhanced by the failure to provide adequate counsel and the narrowing of the opportunity to raise the issue of innocence on appeal. Once an execution occurs, the error is final.

PART THREE

FAMILIES

18

They Sentenced My Son to Die

Shirley Dicks

As I looked out the window from the third floor of the small jail, I could see into the room where the twelve jurors were sitting. They were laughing loudly and I had to wonder at how these people could be so merry when they were deciding if my eighteen-year-old son Jeff was going to live or die.

Time stood still, my heart was racing, and I wanted to jump out of the window and take my son and run—run far away from the state of Tennessee, run to a place where my child would be safe. He was not guilty of murder. He had never hurt anyone in his life. "Oh God, how can you let this happen?" I screamed. Grabbing the bars with my hands, I tried to bend them, but it was useless.

Suddenly I saw the back door of the courthouse open. My oldest daughter Tina came outside, her head bent low, her long, brown hair covering her face. I yelled down to her, "Tina . . . what happened?" Tina looked up at me, and then she ran. I knew in that instant that the jury had chosen death. My son who had never hurt anyone would die in Tennessee's electric chair. He would die for a crime he never committed.

"No . . ." I screamed. "Nooo . . . you can't do that to my son . . . oh God no. Not my son." The room was spinning, my chest seemed to hurt and I couldn't breathe. Taking hold of the bars, I felt the screams keep on and on until through a fog I heard my mother's voice.

"Shirley, please stop. This isn't the end, we'll fight it. Please . . . Shirley, your father. Think of your father." I looked over at Pop as he stood there, his snow-white hair shining in the afternoon sun. Tears rolled down his face and I knew with his heart trouble, he couldn't take much more of it. I had to find the strength to stop. He looked up at me and I loved him so much. I loved my son too and now the state was taking him away. Taking him to die a terrible death in the electric chair.

I saw Detective Keesling walk out of the courthouse, and he smiled up at me, an evil smile. Then he looked at my mother and father and told them to get out. He had no sympathy for them. He had won. I watched as Mar and Pop looked back, tears and despair on their faces, and with shoulders slumped, they slowly turned and walked away.

I backed away from the window and began screaming again. They couldn't kill my child. I wouldn't let them take my son and kill him. It wasn't long before a nurse came in with my mother and gave me a shot. Mar told me that they were going to release me in the morning. I had been given ten days in jail for crying out in the courtroom. As darkness overcame me, I thought back to when I first got the phone call from Jeff.

Jeff had called me and asked me to come to Tennessee as fast as I could. "I need you mom," he said. I knew from the tone of his voice that something bad had happened, and I told him I'd be there as soon as I could. It was a two-hour drive from Asheville, North Carolina, where I lived with my husband and my other three children.

When I got to the hotel room where Jeff was waiting with his pregnant wife, I saw how pale his face was. Betty sat there while Jeff told me what had happened. He and Donald Strouth had been out riding, with Jeff driving the car. Donald, or "Chief," as he was called, told Jeff to pull over in front of a used clothing store. Jeff did as he was told, and Chief said he was going to rip the store off.

Jeff just laughed and didn't believe that he would do it. Chief got out of the car and walked into the store. Jeff waited, sure that Chief would come back outside laughing. But five or six minutes went by, and Jeff was getting scared. He wondered if Chief was indeed robbing the store. Suddenly he saw Chief come running back to the car, his pants and hands covered in blood.

"My God, what happened?" Jeff asked. Chief told him to get going and he did. Jeff found out later that Chief had robbed the man in the store of $200 dollars and hurt him. Chief asked Jeff if he wanted any of the money, and Jeff said no. He didn't want anything to do with the robbery. Later on the news Jeff found out the man had been killed.

I didn't know what to do, so I hid them out for a couple of weeks, until Jeff decided he wanted to turn himself in because he was not guilty. He hadn't taken part in the crime, he had taken none of the money, and whatever they gave him, he would take.

I went with Jeff to the police station where a detective read him his rights. We hardly listened since we had not had any dealing with the police before. Detective Keesling was from Tennessee and he said we would not need an attorney present. He took Jeff into another room where Jeff gave a statement. Unfortunately, we didn't know any better, so I let Jeff give that statement. He told the truth, that he was there in the car, had not known Chief would actually rob and kill anyone. To our horror, Jeff was charged with first-degree murder. Fear overwhelmed me.

Jeff was taken to Bluntville, Tennessee. Every weekend I traveled eighty miles from our home in North Carolina to Tennessee. The trip was hot over a winding road. I was pregnant, as was Jeff's wife.

In the jail Jeff lost weight, his eyes became sunken into his face, and he looked like a war prisoner. Hard as I tried to hold myself together in front of Jeff it was next to impossible. He was my child, my first-born child, and he was being mistreated. It was a nightmare.

I spent all my energy trying to raise money for Jeff's defense. I found out that attorneys wanted $100,000 to represent him because he had made a statement without an attorney, and this was going to be a capital trial. They were going for the death penalty. They already had Chief in custody and knew he had done the killing. However, they wanted both of them to die.

I put my home up for sale but couldn't get much for it as we had only had the home for eight years. I wrote to all the famous attorneys and found that they wanted millions to represent Jeff. No one would help us. We were nobody. We were not rich. Who cared if an innocent boy died for a crime he did not commit?

The prosecution arranged for Jeff and Donald to be tried separately, so that both could get the death penalty. I wasn't aware then that testimony in Chief's trial was not allowed at our trial as it was called hearsay. Therefore, our jurors did not hear the whole thing. This is something that I can't understand, why the judge can pick what the jurors can and cannot hear. They do not hear the whole trial, the testimony of everyone, only what the judge says they can hear. How can they be expected to come back with a fair verdict when they do not hear the whole thing?

Chief had his trial first and Betty and I went over to Tennessee. Betty had to testify against Chief, as did his girlfriend Barbara Davis. Barbara had taken police to where Chief had buried his bloodied jeans and told them what Chief told her. That he had killed the old man. He had bought a used car for the two hundred dollars and the used car salesman was in the court-room and also testified. Jeff McMahan, a friend of Chief to whom he had gone after the murder, also testified that Chief had blood on his jeans and had told him that he killed someone. He told McMahan that his partner took no part, but had frozen up in the car. Chief was found guilty and sentenced to die.

I knew at that point that my son would also die if I couldn't get him an attorney. A court-appointed one had been assigned to him, but I didn't trust in them because they do not get very much money, and James Beeler, the man who was going to be Jeff's attorney, told us that he had never handled a capital case before. Looking back, I wish I had let him go on, but I was intent on getting a paid attorney to give my son a better chance.

I couldn't raise enough money for an attorney so I decided to break him out of the small jail where they were holding him. My husband said I was crazy, and I guess I was at that point. All I knew was they wanted to kill my son and I had to save him. I had to save him at any cost . . . and if it meant I would go to jail, then that was all right too.

I planned the jail break and talked to a couple of guys who said they would help me. In reality they took the papers to the police and told on me. They moved Jeff to Brushy Mountain prison in Knoxville, Tennessee, where there was no way I could ever get him out. I was lucky that they didn't bring charges against me.

My next crazy thought was to write checks and buy mer-chandise, then sell it at the flea market. It took me three times before I was able to learn how to do that right, and I began to buy things. My daughters were scared when I told them what I planned on doing, but I felt it was the only way. Jeff would die unless I found him competent counsel.

I lost my baby in the seventh month of pregnancy. It had been a boy, and in my mind I thought God was telling me that Jeff would live. That he was taking this new baby and giving it to someone else, and allowing me to have my first son.

Betty gave birth to a little girl whom they named after me, but we called her Maria, her middle name. She was beautiful, and we took her to the prison to see her father. Jeff looked at her with such love it brought tears to my eyes. I knew how much he loved her, he had always loved children.

Betty had begun to be abusive to Maria, and the baby was in the hospital a few times from this abuse. Betty was going to give her up to an orphanage in Knoxville, and I told her that no way was she giving up my son's child. I would adopt her and raise her as my own. That way Jeff could be a part of his daughter's life. She signed her away and told how she abused her, how she couldn't raise a child and didn't want her. I legally adopted Maria.

I wrote checks and was able to hire an attorney. His name was Larry Smith from Asheville, but I didn't know at the time he was only interested in the money. He knew how I was getting the money because I told him, and he said he would let me know when the warrants would come in. I knew I would have to serve time, but it was a small price to pay for my son's life.

During the trial, testimony was changed from the first one. The jurors didn't hear that Chief was the triggerperson in the beginning. They never called on Jeff McMahan to testify. I had talked to him during Chief's trial and he said he would come to our trial if I could pay his way over. He didn't have the money to do that. I agreed, but our attorney didn't call on him. The judge didn't let the jurors see Chief when we called him to the stand, and he stood on the Fifth Amendment.

The medical examiner changed his testimony also. From the first trial where he said the victim was unconscious on the floor as Chief stood over him and slit his throat, the blood spurting upward on the bottom of Chief's jeans, he now said that a very strong man could have held him in an upright position while Donald slit his throat. Why no one even questioned that the blood would have been on Chief's shirt and not on the bottom of his jeans if that was the case, I don't know. I hadn't been allowed in the courtroom, but during closing arguments they let me in. When they were lying, I yelled out so the jurors could hear, but the judge ordered me locked up.

Jeff was given death and moved to Nashville, Tennessee, where he was the eleventh person on death row. Warrants against me were in and I had to run with my youngest son who was twelve and Maria. We were on the run for a year until I had to go back to see Jeff. I told the FBI I would come in if I could see my son at least one time. I was lucky in that I only got probation and was able to move to Tennessee to be with Jeff.

The years rolled on, and Maria, Trevor, and I lived in a small town near Nashville. There we would visit Jeff every weekend. I ran into Betty when Maria was twelve years old and decided that maybe she had changed, so I let Maria get to know her. Betty had left Jeff in the very beginning and was living with another man.

She started visiting Jeff again, but then I realized she hadn't changed at all. She was mentally abusive to Maria and tried to come between her and her father. Betty and Jeff were remarried and she tried to drive us away, but we stayed. I knew she had a mental problem: she had told so many lies about me—that I had stolen her child—to anyone who would listen. She continued to live with Jimmy even though married to Jeff, and soon she stopped visiting again. Maria was having problems because of her, and we had to get counseling for her.

I took Maria out of school when she was fifteen and she stays with me all the time. I began writing books about capital punishment and sold my life story called *They're Going to Kill My Son.* This is the whole story of what happened because you can't get it in one chapter. I started a ministry for those on the row and began speaking out against the death penalty. I found out about many people who had been executed and had been innocent.

We in the United States have sentenced over 350 people wrongly and have executed over twenty-five innocent people in this century. It doesn't seem to matter to some people, they don't care how many people have to die if we kill a few guilty. Since we have over twenty thousand murders a year and fewer than two hundred go to death row, the death penalty is not a deterrent. It is not given out fairly, only to the poor. I have devoted my life to fight the death penalty and hope that my son will be spared. I found out that no one really cares about us. We are not rich and famous. I have written to thousands of famous people begging for help, to attorneys, to movie stars, to everyone who is anybody, but no one will help. I have written to the past three presidents, with no answer . . . no help.

I have been on a couple of talk shows as I have written five books on capital punishment. The big shows like "Oprah" and "Donahue" have called me but want Jeff to go on with me. He will not, because every time an inmate goes on television they make mincemeat of him. He doesn't want to do that to help ratings in a show. He says they don't care, and I believe it. Until I can get enough books sold, get money, my son will sit there, unless they kill him, and I won't let that happen.

We lost my father seven years ago. He never lived to see

Jeff free. Now my mother is ill with emphysema. I have been diagnosed with heart disease and can only pray that God will let me live long enough to see my son walk out of that prison, a free man.

If I could change places with my son I would do it. I die a little each day, just knowing what could happen if we lose in our appeals. Sometimes I am hopeful, then other times it seems as if it's a losing battle. People don't want to be our friends, because we have a loved one in prison. Kids tease Maria and won't play with her because her father is on death row. It's been a hard time for all of us. If people would only understand that we are also victims—victims of a system that says the families of death row inmates are no good and should hide away from the rest of the public. But I am not quiet, I speak out everywhere I go.

I was able to go on death row and make a video for teenagers of death row inmates talking to them. We show the electric chair and it seems to make a difference to the kids. I speak to them after they see the film and I know it has made a difference in a lot of them. If I can reach kids before they get into trouble, then my life will have meaning again. The video is called *The Choice Is Yours* and can be purchased from my group called Tennessee Friends Outside, PO Box 321, Murfreesboro, TN 37130. The cost is $20 per video, and I feel it should be in all schools and every home that has a teenager in it.

If I could live this painful experience again, I would tell my son to run. I wouldn't put my trust in a justice system that murders juveniles, the mentally retarded, and innocent people in the name of justice. This isn't like "Perry Mason" where the good guy goes free. This is the real world where innocent people are killed by the state and will continue to be killed until the death penalty is abolished, as it has been in every other civilized country.

19

The Power of Forgiveness

Bill Pelke

On May 14, 1985, four ninth-grade students from Lew Wallace High School in Gary, Indiana, decided to skip school during their lunch hour. They drank some wine and smoked a joint. They began to think about what they would do for the rest of the day. They wanted to play video games at the local arcade but they didn't have any money. April Beverly came up with an idea. "There is an old lady who lives catercorner across the alley from me. She teaches Bible lessons and she lives alone. I think she has money. If you three go knock on her door and say you would like to take her Bible lessons, she will probably let you into her home. Then you can rob her. Since she would recognize me, I'll stay outside as a lookout."

The three other girls, Denise Thomas, Karen Korders, and Paula Cooper, knocked on Ruth Pelke's door. She answered it. Bible lessons. She invited them into her home. Ruth Pelke was seventy-eight years old and for all of her life had been faithful not only to the many services that her church offered, but also to the Bible lessons that she taught to the neighborhood children. I remember her telling those stories when I was a child thirty-five to forty years ago. She taught youngsters through a program called Child Evangelism.

Ruth used a flannel graphboard and cut-out pictures to represent Bible characters. This helped the children visualize the stories as she would tell them. I remember especially the stories of Joseph: how his coat had many colors and how his jealous brothers had sold him into slavery. I remember the stories of David, the shepherd boy who slew the giant Goliath and how he later became the King of Israel. I remember the stories about Jesus and His disciples. Ruth Pelke was my grandmother. To our family she was known as "Nana."

At the age of seventy-eight, Nana did not have many opportunities to tell children about Jesus anymore, so she welcomed the chance to witness to these young girls. As Nana turned her back to get information for them, one of the girls grabbed a vase from an end table and hit her over the head. As Nana fell to the floor, Paula produced a twelve-inch butcher knife and began to stab her.

April and Karen began to ransack the house, looking for money. They weren't finding much. Paula began to look for money while Karen took over with the knife. Karen held the knife in Nana. April left her look-out post and joined in the search for money. The girls ended up with about ten dollars and Nana's ten-year-old car. Several of the girls drove in the car back to Lew Wallace High School and took other classmates joyriding. Nana died. Two days later, the girls were arrested for their role in the crime.

The date set for the sentencing hearing for Paula Cooper was July 11, 1986. The other three girls had already been sentenced for their roles in the robbery/murder. April Beverly, the neighbor girl who had set Nana up, received a twenty-five-year sentence. Denise Thomas was sentenced to thirty-five years. Denise was accused of being the one who hit Nana in the head with the vase. She was only fourteen years old when the crime was committed. Karen Lorders was sentenced to sixty years. Karen was accused of turning and twisting the knife in Nana for fifteen to twenty minutes.

The prosecution had sought the death penalty for Karen, but the judge deemed that Karen was under the influence of a dominating person, Paula Cooper, and elected not to sentence her to death. There was no jury; it was the judge's call.

Paula Cooper's sentencing hearing lasted about four hours. It is a day I will never forget. Things that happened that day will forever be etched in my mind. I had not been to the trials of the first three girls but, for some reason, I felt like I needed to take off work and be there for Paula's. If Paula was to be sentenced to death, she would be the youngest female on death row in America. Because Paula was only fifteen, I didn't think the judge would sentence her to die.

The prosecution argued strongly for the death penalty. They insisted that the judge sentence Paula to death for her part in the heinous crime. Paula was accused of stabbing Nana thirty-three times. Paula's attorney, a public defender, argued for her life to be spared. Paula had pled guilty, and there had been no plea bargain for a lesser sentence.

I watched as my father testified for the prosecution. He spoke of the circumstances of finding Nana's body. I watched as he reviewed pictures of the crime scene. What my father saw when he discovered Nana's body, they say, is something no man should ever have to bear. For him to live that same scene over and over again in his mind was continued torture. My dad was able to bear that heavy load with God's help through five different trials and hearings. I watched and I listened to many things that happened that day. Most I will never forget. The bottom line for the sentencing hearing and the newspaper headlines the next day was what stood out most, "COOPER SENTENCED TO DEATH."

November 2, 1986. Life goes on. The murder and trials were put on a back burner. My personal life was about to explode. My girlfriend Judy and I had broken up about six weeks earlier by mutual agreement. Although we had dated for quite some time we were both agreeable to move on in different directions. Shortly after the breakup, I began to realize that was not what I really wanted. I began to see that I loved her a whole lot more than I had ever realized, and I missed the relationship that we once had, and I wanted it back.

Judy did not see it that way. She loved me a lot and had enjoyed the relationship, but she did not feel it was going anywhere. She was beginning to enjoy the freedom of being unattached and did not want to get involved in another steady relationship with me. That broke my heart.

When I drove to work in 1986, I was brokenhearted. For the three weeks leading up to this day, I had been doing something I hadn't done very often for the past ten years. I had been doing a lot of praying. It was the only way to find any peace. I had to pray to keep my sanity. I was stumbling in deep depression. God was the only one I could talk to, cry to, and share my burdens with.

I asked God why my life had been so hard. Why this broken heart? I began thinking about my grandmother's death. It all came off of the back burner. I asked God why had he permitted one of his most special angels to die such a horrendous death. Why did our family, a good family, have to suffer the pain that we all had endured? Why? Why? Why?

I had been in tears since I had first started praying about my separation from Judy, and as I thought about Nana, the tears were flowing down my cheeks, and I could only ask God why. While wallowing in my own self-pity, I suddenly pictured somebody with a whole lot more problems than what I had. I pictured Paula Cooper. I pictured a young girl, slunk in the corner of a death row cell, with tears in her eyes and looking up to nowhere in particular, moaning, "What have I done? What have I done?" My mind flashed back to the day Paula was sentenced to death. Her parents were not even there for this most important day in her life. I recalled Paula's grandfather at the trial. As the judge was in the middle of delivering his sentence, the old man began to cry and wail, "They're going to kill my baby, they're going to kill my baby." The judge ordered the bailiff to remove him from the courtroom, as it was disrupting his court. I saw the tears running down his cheeks as he was led from the courtroom.

I recalled that as the trial ended, Paula was led away to death row. There were tears running down her cheeks and on to her light blue prison dress, causing dark blotches all over the front of her dress. There is a very beautiful picture that was taken a year and a half before my grandmother was killed. Whenever the media did a story about Nana's murder, the subsequent trials, and Paula's death sentence, they used that particular picture. As I sat I envisioned an image of Nana, in the likeness of that photograph but with one distinct difference. I pictured Nana with tears streaming out of her eyes and rolling down her cheeks.

I had been in tears for about fifteen minutes as I had been crying and praying, but when I pictured Nana's tears it deepened my pain tenfold. I knew those tears of Nana's were tears of love and compassion for Paula and her family. I know that

Nana would not have wanted the grandfather to go through the death row scene. Paula's uncle and sister were at the trial and also pleaded for the judge to spare Paula's life. I knew Nana would not want them suffering through Paula's execution. And I knew Nana would not have wanted Paula to be put to death even though Paula had killed her.

I began to think about Nana and her faith in Jesus. I began to think about what Jesus had to say about forgiveness. I was raised in a home and church that taught the Bible and I immediately thought of three incidents that Jesus taught about forgiveness. I thought about the Sermon on the Mount. He taught we must forgive. I also recalled about Jesus talking to his disciples about forgiveness and we should forgive seventy times seven. I knew that meant don't quit forgiving after 490 times. I recalled Jesus when he was crucified, the nails in His hands and feet, and I pictured the crown of thorns in His brow and pictured His looking up to heaven and saying, "Father forgive them, for they know not what they are doing." I felt that Paula did not know what she was doing. Anyone in their right mind does not stab someone with a twelve-inch butcher knife thirty-three times.

I had to admit to myself at that point that forgiveness was the right thing to do and I would try and do that for Nana's sake. Because of her tears, tears of love and compassion. I felt that she wanted someone in our family to have that same love and compassion. I felt like it fell on my shoulders. It seemed too heavy a burden to bear. My tears continued to flow.

Even though I knew forgiveness was the right thing, as far as love and compassion, I had none. After all, my grandmother had been brutally murdered. The chief of police in Gary, Indiana, Virgil Motely said it was the most heinous crime he had ever seen in his thirty-five years on the force. For two years in a row, Gary, Indiana, had been the murder capital of the United States. Motley had seen his share.

Nana's tears dictated to me that I try to generate some sort of love and compassion and so, with nowhere else to turn, I started praying again. In tears I begged God to please give me love and compassion for Paula and her family. I begged on behalf of Nana. My next thoughts were that I could write to Paula and tell her about Nana and her faith in Jesus. I thought I could also write about God's love for her, and His forgiveness for her. I even thought I could tell Paula that through Jesus I had love for her.

At this point I realized my prayer for love and compassion for Paula Cooper and her family had been answered. Two things were immediately clear to me. First, I realized what is the most important lesson I have ever learned in my life. When God granted my request of love and compassion, the forgiveness was automatic. It wasn't something I had to do; God did the work. The second was I no longer wanted Paula to die.

When Paula was sentenced to death, I had no problem with it. I knew people were being sentenced to death and being executed around our country. I felt if they didn't give the death sentence in Paula's case, then they were telling me and my family that Nana was not an important enough person to merit the death penalty and I felt my grandmother was a very important person.

I began to think about what others would think. After all, I had just made a 360-degree turn. What would my family think? My father had testified in court that it would be a travesty of justice if Paula did not receive the death penalty. What would my friends think? What would my co-workers think? Many of the people I worked with would say as a means of condolence for Nana's death, "I hope the bitch burns." I knew some were not going to understand how I now felt. I knew it would be the same with friends outside the mill.

But I also knew the beauty of God's love and compassion and the forgiveness it brought. I knew I had done the right thing and I would just try to get the others to understand it. I was sure I was right. From the day of Nana's death until this moment the thought of Nana tore my soul. When I thought of her I pictured her lying butchered on the dining room floor. For fifteen to twenty minutes Karen had twisted and turned the knife in Nana, and in fact the carpet beneath her body was shredded and the hardwood floor was splintered. The thought of Nana butchered tore me up.

Suddenly, after learning the lesson of forgiveness, I began to picture Nana in a beautiful way. The way she lived and what she stood for and who she was. It was such a relief to see her that way. I knew I would no longer picture her butchered on the dining room floor again.

I saw many possibilities arising out of the reasons why God had allowed me this experience. I began praying again and I made God two promises that I have kept to this day. First of all, I knew that I could not take any credit for forgiving Paula. I knew that it was only because God touched my heart.

I began a letter-writing exchange with Paula. I let her know that God cared for her and loved her and that I did too. We exchanged letters about every ten days, and we established that we would like to visit and meet each other. I shared Nana's faith with her. It was difficult to write many of the letters at first, although many tears of joy would often hit the pages. Tears of joy knowing that I could truly love someone who had caused our family such pain. I always prayed to God before I wrote Paula and asked Him to guide me and help me say the right things, the things that needed to be said.

I had the opportunity to meet Paula's grandfather shortly before Christmas. I took a basket of fruit to his house and spent several wonderful hours talking and looking through the old family albums. There were pictures of Paula as she was growing up. She had been a very cute little girl. I had also informed my parents that I was corresponding with Paula. They did not understand why, but my dad did say, "Well, do what you have to do." I thanked him for that.

Anna Guaita called me and explained that she was an Italian journalist and that she and a colleague, Giampalo Palli, were coming to Indiana to do a story on Paula Cooper. There had been unusual reaction in Italy to Paula's case. It made headlines in the Italian newspaper when Paula was sentenced to death. The Italians, who do not have the death penalty, could not understand why the State of Indiana would want to execute a young woman who was only fifteen years old. They could not understand executing a woman at all, and why it was a black girl to get this punishment.

The Italian people were fascinated with this story and Anna and her friend were coming to Indiana to do interviews. Their stories would run in the three largest Italian newspapers. Anna had called the Gary *Post Tribune* and asked for leads to whom they should interview for their story. She was advised about Paula's attorney, her grandfather, several others, and about the grandson of the victim, who had written a letter to the *Voice of the People* and talked about forgiving people, so she wanted to interview me.

Anna turned out to be a great person and we had a wonderful interview. We talked for hours. Their stories about Paula's case, including interviews with Paula, myself, and others, were spread over two days in the Italian papers.

About four months after the night I forgave Paula, Judy and my best friend Wayne were at her house and we were talking about my involvement with Paula. Wayne and Judy had both stood by my side when Nana was murdered. I needed strength and God gave me Wayne and Judy. Wayne and I had worked together for twenty years and throughout the years we have often talked about things relating to the Bible. We often talked about that night. We both firmly agreed that there is no argument according to the Bible. Forgiveness is encouraged, taught, and, if you will, commanded in God's Word.

An Italian television station wanted me to come and do a segment on Paula's case. Of course I jumped at that. One of the reasons I wanted to go was that when Anna had finished the interview with me, she mentioned that over forty thousand people had signed petitions to have Paula taken off death row. I wanted to go and thank each one of them. When the American press found out I was going to Italy, it became a media event.

When I found I was going to Italy, I began to pray and fast. I fasted for about eleven days before I went to Italy. The segment on Paula went very well. They had a poet who had written about her. There was also an elderly Catholic priest, Father Gerganti, who was spearheading a drive by the organization "Don't Kill" (Carcere comunita) to gather signatures on petitions to have Paula taken off death row.

When I arrived home from Italy, Wayne and Judy met me at the airport. They didn't always agree with what I was doing but they were both personal supports and that is what was important to me. Judy and I had kind of got back together at this point and we were both very glad to see each other. Magazines I had never read were now printing my story of forgiveness.

Every several months it seemed like there would be a press conference in Indianapolis for either Paula, her appeal, or for death penalty opponents. I was always invited to attend and speak. At one of these meetings I met Magdaleno Rose-Avila.

He was the death penalty abolition coordinator for Amnesty International USA.

He asked if we would like to go to Atlanta the following weekend and lead the death penalty march that Amnesty International would be having during its annual general meeting. Amnesty International would pay our expenses, so Father Vito and I took him up on it.

About two months after the meeting in Atlanta, I arrived home from a trip to Albany, New York, about 6 A.M. after driving all night with my cousin Judy. I played the answering machine for messages. Picture a tear coming to my eyes as the machine responded, "This is the Oprah Winfrey program and we would like for you to be our guest on the segment, 'Forgiving the Unforgivable.' " I called Wayne and played the message for him. Praise the Lord, it was a miracle.

I didn't tell Judy I was going to be on "Oprah." I was hoping she would be working at the hospital and walk in a patient's room and hear me on the show talking about forgiveness. Judy had said that it would be the sign of a miracle if Oprah ever called. Even though Judy didn't see the show, her sister called her and told her that it had been on. On the show I had been able to talk about Nana, her life and her faith, and about Jesus. It was live—nothing was cut as had been done on most other interviews. I have found out the media doesn't want to quote people when they are talking about Jesus. It was great to be on an uncut program. (It was on "Oprah" that I met SueZann Bosler who has become a wonderful friend. Lo and behold another miracle.)

Judy and I were married on October 1, 1988, and we went to Italy for our honeymoon. Judy's mother was happy to accept our invitation to join us. She had also thought I was crazy for forgiving Paula, so inviting her to Italy made me look a little better as her new son-in-law. It was a dream vacation for her. Judy and I had a wonderful honeymoon. I met many of the friends from my first visit to Rome and we all just had a great time.

This was my third time to Italy, and only the first at my expense. I had also flown to Milan for a television program there in the fall of 1987. While on the honeymoon, quite a few press events took place because of the increasing interest the Italian people had in Paula Cooper. Her case was very well known in Italy, so there was interest in my being there. Judy was very understanding of how I had to go through the open doors. Some days required an amount of time and also distance to travel. On those days Judy would go shopping with her mother, while Father Vito would drive me somewhere for an interview or some other sort of activity. In the evening we would usually gather for dinner and Father Vito would always treat us.

Anna Rita Petrita had us to her home for dinner. Franco and Italo took us for pizza, and Phillipo took us all out to a very unique restaurant. The honeymoon was great. Another special day, a very special day, happened when I was at work. About nine months after we were married, Judy and I were talking on the telephone and she told me there was a beep on her end of the line. She put me on hold for a moment and then came back and said that someone from the Associated Press was on the other line and they wanted to talk to me. I had Judy give them my work number.

The Associated Press had done a very nice story about my involvement with Paula. One of their reporters had met me at a local restaurant a few months after my first trip to Italy. He conducted a very nice, warm interview. It was a good story, complete with pictures, and it had run in newspapers throughout the country. The phone rang at work. The reporter from the

AP informed me that the Indiana Supreme Court had just over-turned Paula's death sentence. She would now serve a sixty-year sentence. The AP wanted a comment from me.

The first thing I said was "Praise the Lord." What a period of rejoicing I went through for a number of days. I was extremely happy that Paula was now off of death row, at least technically. I learned it might be at least another two months before all the paper work would be completed to move her into the general prison population. The pressures of being on death row could now ease up for Paula, although she had learned to handle things very well. About five or six people took Paula under their wing while she was on death row and showed her love and compassion. They all helped Paula plant the seed of hope within herself. She was responding to that love with love.

What about me?

What about missions and messages and such? What about the opportunities to speak of love and compassion, forgive-ness, Nana, and Jesus? I always have had a special love for Jesus ever since I was very little. I am not sure where it came from. My family—mom; dad; and my older sister, Dottie—all loved Him. Where I went to church everybody loved Him, and I knew Nana loved him. Somewhere it all rubbed off on me. I went to Bible college because I loved Jesus.

To be able to speak with authority on love and compassion and know that I had the Bible to back it up was a wonderful and powerful experience. Were those opportunities now gone since Paula was off of death row and her case would cease to be a media sensation? Was my mission over? I surely hoped not. What next?

The Pilgrimage

I did not know who Sister Helen Prejean was when I first heard about the pilgrimage, but she was the inspiration behind it. The Pilgrimage was a march from the death row at Starke, Florida, to the burial site of the late Dr. Martin Luther King, Jr., in Atlanta, Georgia. May 4 to May 19, 1990, would be two weeks of walking and speaking out against the death penalty. The message behind the event was spiritual, and much effort was spent trying to reach the religious community with the torch of this act of conscience.

I felt I needed to be part of two weeks of action against the death penalty for spiritual reasons. After all, spiritual reasons that had gotten me involved in the anti–death-penalty campaign in the first place. Judy had to work, and while she encouraged me to go on the Pilgrimage by myself, she preferred that I would go for only one week instead of two.

After two days of preparation and goodbyes, I filled up my van with gas and began a journey for a destination one thousand miles away, Gainesville, Florida. I knew I would miss Judy, but I was excited about the prospects of once again being able to deliver a message or two about love and compassion, forgiveness, Nana, and Jesus. I didn't know what to expect but I was excited.

There was an execution the day I got there. Jesse Talfero had been electrocuted. It was a botched execution. That first evening there was a service to begin the Pilgrimage. One of the people I met there was Kay Talfero, the mother of Jesse. She was there with Mike Radelet, someone I had met several times before. He introduced her to me as Kay. We hugged and it was as she hugged me that I realized that this must be the mother of the boy just executed. She spoke to us all that night and urged us to go on with our Pilgrimage and said that she knew that

Jesse wanted her to be there that night with us for him. It was one of those moments you don't forget.

The Pilgrimage was so great that I really wished Judy could have been there to see what was going on. When I arrived for the start of the Pilgrimage, I featured my role in this event as that of a servant. I would do whatever I saw that needed doing. I had a vehicle and because of that alone I could be of help in a lot of things. In fact, since my van had a hitch, whenever we caravaned across Florida and Georgia I got to haul the portable pottie.

My van had a citizen's band (CB) radio, as did five of the vehicles that had been rented for the Pilgrimage. With my little outhouse in tow I always brought up the rear. No pun intended. My handle on the CB channel was Port-a-Pottie Bill.

The media was curious as we went from town to town. They wanted to know why a bunch of people would be doing what we were doing. Everybody had a good reason. Sister Helen would always mention to the press that among the marchers were several people who had a family member murdered and yet were here marching and speaking out against the death penalty. She would alternate between sending the press to either Sam Sheppard or myself. Sam's mother had been murdered when Sam was seven years old. The two weeks of the Pilgrimage gave me many opportunities to speak out: press, radio, television, rallies, and church services.

My best talk was at a Wednesday night prayer meeting service at a black missionary Baptist church. A vanload of pilgrims joined the regulars for the service. Every time I mentioned what the Bible had to say about love and compassion, forgiveness, and some of the various teachings of Jesus, the crowd would say amen. I almost got to preaching, I really enjoyed it.

The Pilgrimage grew in numbers as we got closer to Big A. About thirty-two of us were core marchers who were with the

group at all times. When we got to the Atlanta city limits abo-
litionists from around the country were joining us for the last
weekend events. I think the march ended up in Atlanta with
about 350 people.

During the Pilgrimage, I talked Judy into flying to Atlanta
and spending the last four days of the event with us. I was very
happy that she was able to come and meet the wonderful people I had been meeting for the last two weeks. Judy enjoyed
meeting them all and developed close friendships with many.
She also marched down the streets with us, singing and shout-
ing abolition chants. Was I ever happy to see that! Overjoyed
would probably be the better word.

The last night in Atlanta was a major event. About twenty-
five speakers spoke at the grand finale, which was held at the
Ebenezer Baptist Church, the church of the late Dr. Martin
Luther King, Jr.

It was a great honor for me to be one of the speakers to
stand behind the pulpit that Dr. King had spoken from. Holding
in my hand a special Bible that I will someday give to Paula, I
spoke of love and compassion, forgiveness, Nana, and Jesus.
What a great honor.

Dr. King taught many of us that it was okay to dream and
that dreams can come true. I am glad I did not miss a minute of
the Pilgrimage. I am glad that Judy was able to attend and be a
part of it. If she had not been there it would have been hard to
have explained how and why my life had been jolted and once
again given new meaning and direction. The Pilgrimage
changed my life and it changed the lives of many others who
were there. At the conclusion of the Pilgrimage, Rick Halprin
from Texas announced that the following year there would be
a march in Texas against the death penally.

I knew that from April 4 to April 11, 1991, I wanted to be

in Texas. Judy had to work and wasn't going to go this time. I was going to fly and even bought my ticket, but then Wayne decided to come with me, so we took the van and headed out. I was hoping the TASK march would do something for Wayne. It did.

Wayne became so convinced that the death penalty was wrong that within several days of the conclusion of the TASK march, Wayne looked at me and said, "We should do something like this in Indiana." Bingo!

"Indiana, the place to be in '93" was the slogan we tried to leave on the lips of everyone as the TASK march concluded, and everyone went back to their home states. Rick Halprin, the heart and soul of the TASK march, was the first to commit to Indiana in '93, saying he would not miss it for anything. There were two years to plan a major abolition event.

Murder Victims For Reconciliation (MVFR) would host the event. The group MVFR is the key to the mythical lock that says the death penalty is justice for the victims' family.

20

Winning the Battle against Violence

Coby Coffman

Before Elysia was murdered, we had a lot of joy in our house. We were not just surviving, but thriving. Although Elysia was learning disabled and had been raised in a dysfunctional home in her early years, she had gone through the predictable consequences of those problems. It was really neat because now she was sixteen and we'd had two years of really good times with the teenage rigmarole behind us. We still had run-ins—over putting away the dishes, and stupid things like that—but the horrible teenage stuff was done with. She had turned into the most pragmatic, sensible young woman. Far more mature than I.

I remember when I took her to open up her bank account before she was killed. When we went in the bank I had to tell the woman filling out all the paperwork that the young girl sitting across from her was the most incredible human being. She was working full time, and her last paycheck was $264, which is pretty incredible for a teenager going to school full time, staying on the honor roll, and coping with learning disabilities to boot.

There are a lot of things that I could tell you about Elysia: she was a wonderful human being. I got asked a lot after she was killed, what her hobbies were, what did she do? And the really funny thing is, the things she did, she did with us. She painted things, and she and I worked together. She fixed up a place inside the attic where she and I could paint. I came home one night and found our dining-room table gone, because she had taken it to the attic to fix up a place. She and I would stay up there late at night, especially at Christmastime, and paint Christmas ornaments. She did things with us.

The night she was killed, I was getting mad at her because she hadn't called. But I wasn't worried about her, because I just knew she was with her older brother. He's a single father and she spent a lot of weekends with him to give him a break from the two-year-old. They were awfully close and there was no doubt in my mind that she was at Pat's house. I called a couple of times and got no answer, so I thought they had gone out to eat.

I was doing the motherism—you know, the "I'm gonna kill her, she knows not to be over there and not call me, she knows she needs to call me and let me know where she is"—the same old mother stuff that mothers always do. So I really never expected anything, and I had no reason to. She was not the kind of kid you worried about, doing things she shouldn't be doing or going places she shouldn't be going. If she was anywhere, she was with one of her family. Not that she didn't have friends, but she was really shy and her friends tended to be friends at school, but her home life was private. And that's who she was.

I have pictures of Elysia, but none of them of her by herself. Most of the pictures are of her doing things with her little brothers and sisters. It's hard to describe how we came to a point in our lives where things had sort of settled down. We had our lives planned out. I had been in nursing school and one thing she said was "I don't believe you. All the time I was growing up we were poor, and now that I'm about ready to move out, we're going to have money, and I'm gonna leave home and be poor, and you guys will have money. That's why I didn't leave school. I'd be letting the forces of evil win if I quit, so I didn't."

This has been a struggle for me. When I first found out what had happened, the chaplain and I prayed for the boys who had done it. I mean that was our first instinct. But I have a real visceral reaction to Allan Fest when I see him—he's the one who actually pulled the trigger. I think things like "why couldn't he have been a thalidomide baby and been born with no hands so he couldn't have done it?" I don't feel a sense of hatred, I feel . . . sick. It makes me sick that he had such emotional poverty in his life that he needed to gain recognition that way. It makes me sick that those three boys could watch a little girl die and run away and snatch another purse, go to the game room and party. I don't understand that lack of humanity. I can't understand it at all and yet, when I see them I think, "They were born little newborn babies, innocent and beautiful, just like all newborn babies."

I have to think what happened. I'm willing to believe there's a bad seed in 1 percent of the population. Maybe that many got their wires crossed, but for the most part, I have to believe that what happens is children who grow up to be murderers and sociopaths are failed early on. They are not tended to, they are not loved. Kids need just a few things emotionally. They need to feel capable, which means they need to get strokes for things they do well, and recognition for who they are. And they need to feel needed just like grownups do; they need attention. When I was growing up, I got the idea that attention was a dirty word, that if I needed attention, I was weak, I was dirty. So I understand the background that promotes that lack of attention, and I want it stopped.

I really do want it stopped. I don't know what pushes any-one past the point of having any concern for another human life. And I have to believe that a sociopath who can't feel for another human being also can't feel for himself. That's a completely joy-less human being. And how do you punish a completely joyless human being anymore than that? You just can't do it. They're obviously totally removed from God. So I guess I'm not much into punishment. I definitely think those boys need to be incar-cerated. They don't need to be out on the streets ticking like time bombs around other people's children. And I do believe that each individual needs to be addressed the way they are.

Like Richard. Richard could very well have been in that car. He was a friend of theirs. He could easily have been riding with them. I don't know what his reaction would have been, but I do know that he could have been there. But the thing is he wasn't. And I have hugged this young man and hugged him while he cried because he can cry.

I told six kids who came to Elysia's grave that I wanted them to know that she was really dead. What I really wanted the boys who killed my daughter to do, as a part of their learning experience, was to come to the funeral and touch her and see.

People ask me what I want to see done with the boys; do I want to see them dead? I know exactly what I want to happen to them. I want them to go to prison, and while they're there, I want them to have a spiritual experience. I want God to reach down and touch their hearts down in the very depths of their souls. And it's going to have to be really deep to find their souls at this point, and make them realize what it is that they've really done. I want them to stay in prison and help others who will be getting out.

The funny thing about that is that it's the very worst punish-ment I could wish on them because it's a pain like no other; but on the other hand, it's the best thing that could happen to them. Of course I have no control over that, but God could do that.

I've done a lot of speaking at radio and television shows, and schools, and the thing I really want people to know is that things really can change, if each of us as individuals are willing to make a commitment. And one thing I saw really early on, is that people are really aching for a change, a lessening of the violence, though they argue among themselves about what the problem is.

I think one parent who is able to parent is plenty. God designed two-parent homes because parenting is a very tiring job. I think that's why we have two parents, because when one gets absolutely tired, the other one can take over for a while.

I did have a lot of faith before all this happened, but if you want to experience a spiritual crisis, just give this a try. I was very simplistic in my belief that all things work for good for those who love God. I thought everything was fine, and would be fine, but guess what, not necessarily. I guess that's all taken on a new meaning. God gave us a free will and those three boys were exercising their free will when they killed Elysia. The only thing I can do from here is hope that God can take a horrible situation and bring some good out of it. There could never be enough good to justify it, nothing could ever come from it that would justify it for me. But, on the other hand, I feel an obligation for whatever reason because I have been given a voice that people will listen to. I take the opportunity to do that, and the one thing I really want to do is kind of channel people.

I went to one meeting consisting of victims of crime and people who really want change. It was great. But over on one side were people saying, "Well, what we have to do is get rid of the adult bookstores." Then, over on the other side some were saying, "No, we have to have truth in sentencing." And then other people were saying, "No, we have to redo the juvenile justice system." The fact of the matter is, everyone is right. Those are all problems, and there are other problems. But, what I see happening is a sort of umbrella over many groups in different areas. And I really believe that if we're working toward good, good things will happen. And anyway, anyone who is being part of the solution is not being part of the problem.

I'm not a particular proponent of gun control because I don't think that gun control by itself will solve these problems and I think those who do are pretty naive. But, by golly, I would sure rather see somebody who is passionately for gun control out working for it, than to see them sitting at home getting frustrated, exploding at their children, and being part of the problem. This being America, they're never going to get the guns off the streets because there are too many people who are adamant about their right to bear arms, but if it saves two or three lives, then their efforts have been worth it.

Some people think they have nothing to offer. But those same people are sitting there with an empty lap that could hold a child. You know, a three-year-old child who is not being tended to will in ten years be grown up and looking for his importance with a gun. And that can be stopped by one person with an empty lap, taking the time to say, "Hey, you are God's creation," and paying attention. Everybody who wants to be part of the solution can be; it's just a matter of finding out how. And I think that a lot of good people who want to be part of the solution get stuck because they do not know how.

If you have an hour a month to volunteer somewhere, you can spend that hour each month for a year looking for a place to donate that hour. If you don't know the name of an organization, you can't call them. I would like to create a database from the organizations that indicates what their current needs are, what kind of time requirements they have, and what kind of people they can use. Then, people could use the database to find places that can really use them.

If you take a look at people, most of them are good. Most people you meet on the street wouldn't think of hurting you, wouldn't dream of hurting a child, wouldn't think of stealing your purse. The good guys far outnumber the bad guys. So by sheer numbers, if the good guys say, "Ok, I'm going to tackle one person here. I'm going to pay attention to one child. I'm going to pay attention to one problem," by sheer numbers we're going to win this battle.

How could we lose? I don't think it's so hard to get people involved as it is to let them know that they would be making a difference. I don't think that people don't want to help; I think people feel helpless and hopeless. I think they can be convinced that it's not a hopeless situation, and if I have a message, that's it. The only way we'll lose, is if we decide it's too big a struggle. I will talk until I'm blue in the face as long as people want to hear it. And, I've seen changes.

These kids are out speaking in schools now. Six lives completely turned around. Those six lives can touch many, many lives, just by virtue of who they are. The video *The Choice Is Yours* can help. The guys on death row—they are in a position to reach people because I really believe that if you're talking from your heart, it will reach people. Persons speaking from their heart can touch many, many lives. They can make real changes.

I want to go into the schools and talk to the tough guys. I don't want to go in and talk to the little churchgoers. They're not the ones who will influence the others. Not only that, if I could convince them to wear a purple ribbon so that others could see, that would be asking for trouble, and I wouldn't want to do that. It has to start with the tough guys. It has to. I think it can be done. I think that in small groups the tough guys can be reached.

I told these kids they had a responsibility to reach other kids. The other kid really dies, and the ones who do it really do go to jail. Four lives are down the tubes in the heat of the moment because of the availability of guns. If they don't have them, they won't use them.

I think that with violent crimes—murder, aggravated assault, aggravated rape, anything with violence—I think the kids made a decision to hurt someone. I think we need to skip all the juvenile BS and go right on into the criminal system.

The kids who murdered my daughter haven't even been indicted yet—almost six months later—even though there were six eyewitnesses who know exactly what happened, and who did it. We've spent the last six months in juvenile court. How many times does a mother have to hear in graphic detail about the death of her daughter? How many times do I have to know the angle of his arm when he pulled the trigger, and how many times do I have to hear about how she screamed? I don't think I have to hear it that many times.

We have been to juvenile court over seven times, and every time we go, it totally freezes everyone in this household. My husband and I are just paralyzed. It does emotional things that you wouldn't believe. It just wipes us out. Every single time we go to court, it's that way. There's no way to get around it. Now, we start three separate trials, and we go through it all again.

The thing that people do not understand—and if they really knew about the juvenile justice system, they would be up in arms—the truth of the matter is that because the kid who killed my daughter was sixteen years old, there is no juvenile trial. The evidence is presented to a referee, not a judge—the judge never sees the kid. The referee goes over the evidence. They're not convicted. So here the evidence is presented and the referee says, "Well, it's pretty obvious that you killed her. Six eyewitnesses, I think we have to go with culpability here. You seem to be a dangerous sort here: killed this little girl, you already had her money. She didn't do anything, she didn't hit you, she was walking away. I guess we'd better give you the maximum." The maximum is going to a group home for other youth offenders. By law, they get weekend passes after about three months. Countless murders have been committed by kids on furloughs. In the very worst case, the kid is held until he is nineteen. So if you're talking about a kid who is sixteen years old, by the time you count the time he spent in jail, and by the time he gets good behavior for not killing anyone while on furlough, he spends about eighteen months in a group home.

When he gets out at eighteen, he has no record. No one has any right to know that he killed someone. There's something fundamentally wrong with that. They need to be in prison. They are the types who are walking time bombs. They don't need to be out walking with other people's children. They just don't.

I go back over the whole thing, but I couldn't have done anything different. It wouldn't have mattered if we were together. This could still have happened. And she had earned the right to be where she was. She had earned it.

There are a lot of little children out there who are going to grow up to be bad guys if we don't help them right now. The next time we breathe, it's going to be ten years later, and those very children who are running around like hooligans, who are not particularly lovable because they are desperately seeking attention, will be fifteen or sixteen and be big hooligans looking for attention, this time with a gun in their hands to shoot with.

Youth violence—become a part of the solution, or be part of the problem.

21

The Abuse of Power

Betty McCullough

My son Lonzell Green is currently in Pelican Bay State Prison for a murder he did not commit. He's been there for two years, serving a twenty-five-years-to-life sentence. I believe that my son is in Pelican Bay because my family, the McCullough family, is poor, black, and speaks out and fights for what is right.

In July 1991, my son was framed. Lonzell turned himself in to clear his name. The Oakland police charged him with first-degree murder. The trial lasted ten days, including two days of jury deliberations.

There was no real evidence, no murder weapon, no investigation on my son's behalf, not even a lie detector test. The prosecutor's main witness was an ex-con drug dealer. Another witness was yet another ex-con who didn't even see my son at the scene. A final witness changed her story at least three times and even admitted in the courtroom that she lied to the cops. No one asked me where my son was that night.

My brother was part of a 1989 class action lawsuit against the Oakland Housing Authority (OHA) for allowing its police to conduct terror and abuse against its tenants. Four OHA cops are now in prison. During the lawsuit and beginning in 1990, the Oakland police began raiding my mother's house. On each occasion they found no drugs or any evidence of drugs. During a raid, they called the McCullough family "DP" which stand for dirty people.

The police asked my mother to snitch on people in the neighborhood; she refused. My mother, brother, and nieces have been victims of racial remarks made by the police. I cannot help but put two and two together. These events of the past four years are not accidental. I believe that my son's incarceration is a frame-up to attack anyone who stands up for what is right. My twenty-two-year-old son is not a murderer.

Mothers whose sons have been framed or incarcerated for just trying to survive in this country must reclaim them. I have decided to join Mothers Reclaiming Our Children and to establish an Oakland Chapter. Here is what my son says about his ordeal:

> I was falsely accused and convicted in Oakland, California. In January 1991, a person got killed where my grandmother stays. I was nowhere in sight that night. . . . But it turns out since I'm a young black male that I was going to be charged for such a crime. . . . The police picked up two drug addicts. One was a woman named Linda Powell who made a tape stating that she had seen me do the crime.
>
> The first witness the DA called on the stand was Linda Powell. She said she made her story up only because she was using crack and heroin and just got out of jail, and she said what she thought the police wanted to hear so they would let her go. After that, the DA played the taped statement that she gave to the Oakland police to the jury. The jury believed the tape instead of believing her word, what she said on the stand.

My grandmother got on the stand and told the DA she hadn't seen me that entire month. The DA tried to get her to lie and say that she helped me get away from the scene of the crime. Well, I was convicted. Twenty-five to life is what I was sentenced to.

Part Four

Programs and Organizations

22

Tennessee Friends Outside Organization: Reconciliation Ministries

When someone you love is sentenced to prison your whole family is affected. The loss of your loved one to incarceration is emotionally, spiritually, and economically devastating. You are left with many unanswered questions about the judicial system, prison life, what is happening to your loved one, and how your family is to survive. You also run into judgmental attitudes and rejection from society. Friends, relatives, landlords, employers, and congregations can be quick to condemn and cut off family members who continue to love and support their incarcerated loved ones.

You are not alone. There are others who share your confusion and care about the pain you feel. Reconciliation Ministries recognizes that families of the incarcerated are also forgotten victims of crime. Innocent of any wrongdoing, they are often blamed and ostracized by friends and the community. Through individual and family support, assistance, and advocacy, Reconciliation creates an environment where families can support one another to (1) meet their basic physical, emotional, and

269

spiritual needs; (2), strengthen and maintain family bonds throughout the crisis of incarceration; and (3) aid in readjustment upon release of loved ones, thereby reducing repeated incarcerations and making a safer community for everyone.

Children are often very confused and feel left out when a parent goes to prison. You and your family in the free world are busy trying to make ends meet and supporting your loved one in prison. Children may get shuffled around in the process. Your children might feel abandoned, lonely, scared, confused, angry, sad, and guilty. Yes, even guilty. It may sound crazy, but you would be surprised how many kids think, "If only I was a better child, this never would have happened."

If your children don't talk about their feelings, they might act them out, sometimes in destructive ways. They might do poorly in school, wet the bed, get into fights, cry a lot for no reason, steal things, or have bad dreams. You might notice some of these or other new behaviors in your child. These changes in behavior are cries for help; they need to be heard.

When a parent goes to prison or jail, it is important to tell your child the truth about what is happening. It's more frightening for your child not to know; then they are left to imagine what might have happened to mom or dad. Telling them that their parent is away at school or in the army is also dangerous. They will wonder, "Why doesn't Mom or Dad ever come home to visit? Doesn't he/she love me anymore?" Also, when you tell your children one story to protect them from the truth, you have to keep making up more stories to answer their many questions. You are left worrying, "What will happen when the truth does come out? How will my child react? What if someone lets the secret out in a cruel way . . . maybe another child on the school playground?" How would you feel in your child's place? Would you want to hear the truth and talk about it?

One way to share what is happening with your child is to say something like "Mommy/Daddy did something wrong or broke the law. He/she is not a bad person, because she/he did a bad thing. He/she loves you and does not like to be away from you but she/he was sent to prison to be punished." Children can handle the truth. You can tell your child what it's like to visit, what to say to kids at school. Your child will continue to have questions and feelings about his/her parent begin locked up. You may also notice that your child is competing with his/her parent in prison for your time and attention. Oftentimes this will happen when your child is feeling insecure. He/she needs your attention, love, understanding, and honesty more than ever now.

Encourage your children to stay in touch with their Dad or Mom in prison, suggest that they visit their loved one with you, write letters and send holiday birthday cards, or send school work and report cards, photos of themselves, or pictures they have drawn to their parent who is locked up.

Families with a loved one on death row face all the financial, emotional, social, and spiritual hardships that every prisoner's family faces, but there are added burdens as well. Tennessee's Death Row is located in Nashville. The men are held in Unit 2 at Riverbend Maximum Security Institution while the women are held at the Tennessee Prison for Women. The death penalty is the ultimate rejection of society, a statement that others desire the death of someone you love. At times you feel condemned as well. If you live far from Nashville and from other families with a loved one on death row, you are likely to feel isolated and alone. You might have periods of depression and intense anger. You will be angry at the prison, your relatives and friends, your loved one on death row, and the groups that are working with you. These feelings are likely to surface many times over years of waiting.

Your waiting is uniquely horrifying. Whereas other families might be waiting for a release date, you are waiting for an execution date or the unlikely miracle of a life sentence or retrial. For this reason, your waiting is extremely painful.

Your loved one on death row is trying to cope with long periods of isolation, harassment, intense noise levels, and an uncomfortable and hostile environment, along with the fear of living under a death sentence. It is likely that at some point your loved one will say, "Don't come visit me anymore. You would be better off without me." Your loved one is trying to protect you from the nightmare of death row. He may also be giving up hope of anything but his execution. He may want to drop his appeals to escape the waiting. At this time, he will need your love, advice, and attention more than ever.

23

The Reach and Teach
Prison Program

Reach and Teach is a new concept in youth problems with a working philosophy that will continue to grow and develop over time. The primary aims and objectives of Reach and Teach are to address youths about the consequences of (1) dropping out of school, (2) using illegal drugs that lead to other criminal activities, (3) allowing peer groups to influence their decisions, and an array of other factors that may ultimately lead to incarceration. Unlike Scared Straight, Reach and Teach will not use scare tactics in the form of profanity, abusive language, gestures, etc., toward their youth audiences. Reach and Teach will use real-life experiences of men who were once youths but now are, and have been, incarcerated for long periods of time. These men will tell the stories of their lives prior to incarceration and what happens as a result of incarceration. Reach and Teach will strongly stress the importance of education. There seems to be a concomitant revolt against established education by the youth culture of today. Reach and Teach will strongly solicit the support, assistance, and participation of parents, teachers, social workers, youth organizations, agencies, etc., in its endeavor to deter as many youths as possible from a life of incarceration.

It is, no doubt, what parents expect and what youth peers anticipate. All operate to shape the outlook and approach in youths. We believe in Froebel's metaphor; "that a child be nurtured like a plant lest he be choked by the weeds of circumstance" is more true today than ever.

The impetus for this program is the Constitutional Preamble of Freedom Club, Inc. (FCI), where it states in part, "we will also seek to develop programs to reach the children of our society to educate them on why it is important to know and obey the laws of society," and our FCI Youth Motto: "Ignorance of the law is no excuse, so learn the law so you can obey."

1. This program will address topics that lead to criminal activities, such as drug and alcohol abuse, broken homes, the effect of single parenting, peer pressure, and the importance of education.

2. Reach and Teach welcomes parents of youths to attend and participate in the group discussions, regardless of whether the youths are from detention centers, group organizations, schools, colleges, or just one kid who has strayed.

Reach and Teach believes the roles of parents in this program are vital because some of the problems with youths stem from improper communication with their parents.

This program shall consist of three phases with Visitation Gallery being the suggested meeting place.

Phase 1. This phase will consist of a panel of Inmates discussing how, why, and when they became involved in illicit activities and the consequences, followed by some of their experiences since being incarcerated. This will be called the *Reaching Phase.*

Phase 2. This phase will consist of at least a thirty-to-forty-

five-minute tour of the penal institution while the inmate population is on lockdown for count. The group should be escorted
by the Inmate Panelists, Sponsors, Group Therapist, and Security. This phase shall serve as a means to illuminate the positive
and negative reality of life behind prison walls.

The tour site should include, but not be limited too, at least
one housing unit, HSA, and the Program Building. Following
the tour, everyone will eat lunch and then return to the Visitation Gallery for Phase 3 of the program.

Phase 3. This phase will consist of a panelist discussing
how to avoid incarceration, how to say NO to peer pressure, and
how to measure the importance of getting a quality education.
The group, youths, parents, guests, etc., will be allowed to ask
questions and to make comments. This will be the *Teaching
Phase.*

We realize that every youth cannot and will not be deterred
by Reach and Teach. However, if one can be deterred from
entering prison, then we feel the program is beneficial and
worth our effort.

For further information on the Reach and Teach program,
write Freedom Club, Inc., CCA-SCCC, P.O. Box 279, Clifton,
TN 38425-0279.

24

Northwest Youth Outreach

The Austin Office of Northwest Youth Outreach (NYO) is currently located at 5912 W. Division, Chicago, IL 60651. Three programs operate from this location. The first is the Outreach Programs, where the staff work in and around local public schools, as well as the local parks and other locations where youths gather. The services offered to these youths range from education to recreation. The focus of the outreach program is to provide services to those young people who are at risk of substance abuse and those who are experiencing difficulties in school, at home, and with peers.

The Treatment Program provides assessment and individual, group, and family therapy. Trained professional staff are available to counsel youths who are engaged in drug and or alcohol abuse, or who are experiencing other behavioral problems. Special services are provided for parents.

The Prevention Program works to help local young people avoid using drugs and alcohol. Trained professional staff work toward the goal of a drug-free community by training local people to respond appropriately to the problems of youth. Workshops and seminars are provided to school personnel, community groups, parents, and other interested adults. The prevention staff also conduct classroom presentation in targeted schools.

In addition to drop-in centers, NYO offers alternative activities including holiday parties, dances, summer trips, fan fares, and various sports programs. These activities provide youth with positive options.

CHOICES is about having alternatives, making appropriate decisions maintaining supportive relationships, getting second chances. It is a program for youth having minor difficulties with the law, truancy, or substance abuse. Teenagers eligible for this program are those who are experiencing difficulties at school, at home, or with the criminal justice system. Problems addressed will include truancy, substance abuse, criminal activity, and running away.

Teens enrolled in the program will gain better control of their lives, insight into their behaviors, and skills that will aid in future decision making. Parents who participate in the program will gain insight for establishing more effective households and building better relationships with their teenagers.

CHOICES is a six-step process that includes (1) assessment and expectations; (2) teens—introduction and expectations, parents—impacting and change; (3) teens—decisions and consequences, parents—decisions and discipline; (4) teens—relationships and friends, parents—negative spiral; (5) teens—review and alternatives, parents—review and alternatives; and (6) wrap up and recommendations.

25

The Center for Children
of Incarcerated Parents

Children of jailed and imprisoned parents are a unique population. For many years they have been identified as a special group with special needs; yet, little research has been done on these children and there are very few services for them.

Eight out of every ten jailed or imprisoned women are mothers, and incarcerated mothers have an average of 2.4 children each. Since there are over 75,000 women in jails and prisons nationwide, this means that there are at least 145,000 children of incarcerated women. Altogether, there are over 1,300,000 children of prisoners in the United States.

Children of incarcerated fathers live most often with their families. About 90 percent live with their natural mother or their father's partner; another 8 percent live with their grandparents. Only a small number live with unrelated foster parents or otherwise outside of their natural families.

Children of incarcerated women have more placement problems, since most women prisoners were single parents before their arrests. Only one in five of these children live with

279

their father or with their mother's partner. About 40 percent live with a grandparent, usually the mother's mother.

In most ways children of incarcerated parents are similar to other children from the same social and economic background. Most prisoners had no or low incomes when they were arrested. Very little useful research has been done on the health of children of incarcerated parents. The exception is in the area of perinatal health.

There are patterns of behavior that are typical of children of incarcerated parents. Like other children who have lost a mother or father, these kids usually grieve for their missing parent. In addition to sadness, they may exhibit withdrawal and/or depression. These children may be described as unresponsive and not interested in things. Anger appears in various ways. Some of these children may act out aggressively. Caregivers and incarcerated parents often report hostility, fighting, and rebelliousness, especially in boys. Other children may display anger through lying and stealing. Another behavioral trait is anxiety. Anxious children are hyperactive and overalert. They are very sensitive to stress and overreact to separation from loved ones. Attention problems also emerge in their behaviors. Children of prisoners are often distracted by thoughts of their absent parent; some seem bewildered and confused. Sleep problems like insomnia, nightmares, and night terrors are also common.

Not surprisingly, children with these behaviors have problems in school. The performance of most children gets worse after their parent is arrested. Although a small number of prisoners' children do better in school after mom or dad goes away, most develop further performance problems. Children may be too overwhelmed with what's going on at home to perform well. They don't pay attention in school, don't do their work, and perform poorly on tests. There are several possible explanations for their learning problems, including learning disabilities such as attention disorders and prenatal drug exposure. Poor school attendance often results from children having problems at home, or having performance and learning disabilities. Children of prisoners usually have one or more of these. If these problems are severe enough, children go on to fail or drop out of school.

It appears that children of prisoners are at high risk for entering the criminal justice system. Some studies have identified antisocial behavior in a majority of these children. According to Aid to Imprisoned Mothers in Atlanta, Georgia, children of incarcerated parents are five to six times more likely to go to jail or prison than the average child. This finding is supported by other studies showing that up to 60 percent of the sons of criminal parents become delinquent.

26

Phoenix Youth at Risk

Thousands of young people in Phoenix are in serious trouble. They are failing in school or have been expelled. They are dangerously violent. They break the law. They fight with their families and peers. They are strung out on drugs or alcohol. Quite literally, the lives and the futures of these young people are at risk. Despite the hopes and efforts of parents, teachers, counselors, and others, the youth-at-risk phenomenon is becoming an epidemic. This is not the way it has to be, not for our children and not for our community. The greater Phoenix Youth at Risk Foundation is determined to make a difference, with your help.

Phoenix Youth at Risk is making a difference. It is committed to making an impact on juvenile delinquency in our community. We know there are no easy answers, no quick solutions. But it has been clearly demonstrated that this program does make a difference in helping troubled youths begin to see for themselves how they can lead powerful, committed, and successful lives.

Phoenix Youth at Risk is an autonomous, community-oriented, volunteer-intensive, prevention-intervention program designed to redirect the lives of at-risk youths, and to create an ongoing community response to the growing problem of juvenile delinquency. This grass-roots, nonprofit agency was founded in 1987 by a group of community leaders unwilling to stand by and watch as an entire generation of youths drowned in hopelessness. In 1991, Phoenix Youth at Risk expanded by launching a satellite program in Tucson.

All of the programs of the Greater Phoenix Youth at Risk Foundation are grounded in its cornerstones: possibility, commitment, responsibility, support, community, and integrity. The programs at Youth at Risk have evolved into several primary areas.

New Pathways

New Pathways programs begin with an intensive residential experience combining in-depth educational training and personal redirection through self-examination and athletic challenges. During the residential intervention, participants are involved in lengthy interactive discussions, physical exercise, a ropes course, and Native American healing practices. This course demands a high level of integrity, mutual trust, and communication. Adults affiliated with collaborative agencies also take part in the course, receiving extensive training that they then carry back to the workplace, affecting numerous additional youths.

New Pathway's second component is a six-to-twelve-month program of weekly workshops that pairs each youth with a trained adult volunteer from the community. Together, they set up goals for the youth and establish the intermediary steps necessary to accomplish those goals.

Crossroads

Crossroads projects focus on a specific high-risk community and its youth, with an initial intensive nonresidential phase. Youths in this course experience similar conversations as in residential courses, but are generally a younger population than those in residential courses. Volunteers for nonresidential courses are drawn primarily from the focal community, emphasizing the importance of the community's role in our youths' future. Extensive, professional teacher and helping training takes place, allowing not only the students participating in the programs to benefit from the program, but also all students coming into contact with these adults. As with residential courses, a follow-through program involves trained volunteers who act as mentors to these youths. The format for workshops in both Crossroads and new Pathways programs is based on an educational and skill-building curriculum.

Beyond the Wall

The term "beyond the wall" is a metaphor for going one step farther than you believe is possible for yourself. This concept is emphasized in short-term residential programs called Beyond the Wall. Through coursework, experiential learning, and safe recreation, youths in these programs begin to see possibilities, form goals for themselves, and both look at and begin to release the anger and pain in their lives. Beyond the Wall was piloted in the Creighton Middle School in 1993, and has formed the basis for programs in the Garfield neighborhood, where Phoenix Youth at Risk services began in 1994.

I'm for You

I'm for You programs introduce youth to the cornerstones of Phoenix Youth at Risk, through multiple short sessions and one full day of coursework and experiential learning, with an emphasis on support and trust. This training allows students to understand the concepts of compassion and appreciation for others and for themselves.

Parent Programs

The majority of programs now implemented by the Greater Phoenix Youth at Risk Foundation now include a companion parent program. Parents of youths involved in our programs have the opportunity to meet weekly for workshops that offer education, skill building, and support. Parent programs are a key element in providing a multilevel support structure for youths who are attempting to make positive changes in their lives.

In addition to the cited programs, we also provide extensive volunteer training and helping-professional training. Hundreds of community volunteers have been trained and have participated in all aspects of program delivery, volunteer training, agency operations, evaluation, and fundraising. We have found that volunteers incorporate their training, education, and experience with Phoenix Youth at Risk into their participation in other nonprofit organizations, employment and professional environments, and government settings. Through mutual contributions of both youths and volunteers, Phoenix Youth at Risk pursues a vision of broad community empowerment. To date all programs are provided at no cost to the youths or their families.

For further information, contact Phoenix Youth at Risk, 202 E. McDowell, Sta. 151, Phoenix, AZ 85004 (602-258-1012).

CONCLUSION

27

Juvenile Violence

Shirley Dicks

Our children are killing each other, and the incidence of juvenile crime is rising all the time. With drugs and gangs everywhere, it sometimes isn't safe to walk outside our own homes. What is the answer to this growing problem? How can we rescue our children from this menace?

Teenage violence is escalating at such an alarming rate in Mobile County, Alabama, that officials have termed it a "crisis." Statistics from Mobile's juvenile court show that teens are committing more violent crimes today than they did twenty years ago. The numbers also indicate that guns are the main weapons used by teens charged with violent crimes.

In April, fifteen-year-old Michael Calhoun was charged with the shooting death of thirty-one-year-old Octovia Kendrick, who was robbed and killed while delivering a pizza in Prichard. Sixteen-year-old Andre Turner was charged with the stabbing deaths of Ollie Richardson, sixty-one, and her nephew, LC Bolar, in their Reynolds Avenue home. Both Calhoun and Turner have been ordered to stand trial as adults, charged with *capital* murder—murder possibly punishable by death in the electric chair.

"It's sheer rage. These kids are crying out for help. It's almost as though we have to write this generation of youngsters off because the problem is so bad," said Nancy Winfree, a probation officer and counselor at James T. Strickland Youth Center. "Parents sometimes become so involved in their own pain, they fail to see the child's pain. They expect their children to be adults and they're not."

From January to June 1994, two Mobile, Alabama, juveniles were charged with capital murder, six were charged with murder, thirty-four were charged with armed robbery, and more than one hundred were charged with some type of assault. "When I first came on the bench, we might have one to two murders a year. Now, we're seeing ten to fifteen a year. We are seeing more violent crimes," said Mobile Juvenile Court Judge John Butler.

In 1991, 8,416 complaints were filed in juvenile court and 5,281 of those complaints involved crimes. Those numbers compare with 800 complaints filed in 1976. The growing juvenile crime problem is attracting the attention of elected officials in Alabama.

Attorney General Jimmy Evans attempted to get a bill passed that would automatically remove from the juvenile courts youths sixteen years old and older who are charged with violent crimes and place them in the adult court system. The bill passed the Alabama House, but died in the Senate. Judge Butler said that juvenile court judges across the state supported the legislation and they will try again to get the bill passed. According to Butler, the maximum amount of time a juvenile offender spends locked up in a detention facility is one year—"an inappropriate sentence for someone who has murdered someone."

Many of these kids need help, both in getting off drugs and getting into psychological counseling. However, if these juveniles or their parents lack the money or insurance to pay for treatment, then they do not get help. Youths who finally decide to get off drugs to clean up their lives, need *immediate* help. Without that help they are back on the streets, paying for drugs by committing the crimes that put them in prison.

Yet if the government would put more money into helping kids get off drugs and alcohol, and less into imprisoning them we might see a decline in juvenile crime. If some of the billions of dollars sent overseas each year went into building more therapeutic havens for our kids here in the United States, perhaps they could turn their lives around.

My youngest son had a bad drug habit; he used pot, cocaine, and anything he could get his hands on; he stole from his own family to buy more drugs. When he hit rock bottom and was ready to enter drug rehab, we could barely find him help. If we hadn't "known someone" who took pains to help him, he would never have gone into the rehabilitation program because his family had neither insurance, nor the thousands of dollars that treatment costs. But my son did get help, and today he has been off drugs for a year. Without that therapeutic intervention, who knows what he would have done to pay for those drugs?

Money—or the lack of it—lies at the root of much juvenile crime. A young mother trying to raise her children alone finds the cost of child care out of reach. Making minimum wage, she cannot pay a babysitter to watch her children, so the kids are left alone and to their own devices. They run the streets, get involved in gangs and drugs, and sooner or later become our young criminals. Free or reduced-rate child care would result in less crime because the kids wouldn't be out on the streets unsupervised.

Today, America is not as safe a place to live as it was in the

1950s. In every city and state, we have young children who go to bed hungry, who learn to steal to fill those stomachs. These children learn they have to take care of themselves because no one else will. No one else cares.

In 1991, 5,356 people under the age of nineteen were killed by guns, or almost fifteen youths a day, according to government statistics. Thousands more were wounded by firearms. "This is a critical issue for kids. It's one of the leading causes for children losing their lives today," said Lawrence A. McAndrews, president of the National Association of Children Hospitals and Related Institutions.

The association's survey examined discharge records from forty-four acute care children's hospitals and found that children wounded by gunfire ran up bills that averaged $14,434 in 1991. That is just about what four-year private colleges charged for tuition, room, and board that same year. The association counted only the hospital charges not doctor bills or the costs of lifetime rehabilitation for the wounded.

Some gunshot victims required hundreds of thousands of dollars of care; others were sent home after being stitched up in the emergency room. "We'd a lot rather see that money spent on educating these kids than treating them for gunshot wounds," said Mr. McAndrews, former chief executive of Children's Mercy Hospital in Kansas City, Missouri. He recalled that when polio killed 3,152 adults and children in 1952, it sparked a massive global effort to combat that epidemic, "Here in our own back yard we're losing over 5,000 kids a year and people just shrug it off," said a hospital leader.

A separate study by the U.S. Centers for Disease Control and Prevention found that 59 percent of the youths killed by guns in 1990 were victims of homicide, 30 percent were suicides, and 11 percent unintentional shootings. "Gunshot wounds are the fifth leading cause of accidental death for children under fourteen, and they are the leading cause of death for black teenage boys," Mr McAndrews said. He observed that the children's hospitals are struggling to cope not only with the trauma of treating the wounded, but also with the problem of maintaining security in their emergency rooms. "Not only do we see kids coming in with gunshot wounds, but we see a large number of kids coming in with guns," he said. "That creates a good deal of anxiety and security issues for hospitals and hospital staffs."

In Houston, Texas, teens are three times more likely to be wounded or shot to death than the average resident. They also do more of the shooting. In one month alone, at least eleven Houston teens were killed and ten others rounded up as murder suspects, according to police.

"Kids don't have a conscience because they are not taught to have a conscience," said Homicide Lt. Greg Neely. "Many of them have no remorse because they don't value life." Two out of three children wounded or slain by guns in 1990 were black. Although reasons for juvenile homicides vary, many investigators blame the influence of crack cocaine, violence in television and movies, the breakdown of the family and society, and the emergence of weapons as a status symbol. "It is not uncommon to hear a youth say he bought a gun for $5 on the streets," said Elizabeth Godwin, chief of the Harris County district attorney's juvenile division. "Guns represent both power and a shield from danger," Ms. Godwin said. Many teens just feel that because everybody else seems to have a gun, they had better carry one too.

The number of slayings was up in Houston in 1992. On a rural road, late on New Year's Eve, a motorist fires a single shot into a passing vehicle. Sixteen-month-old Billy Brown, asleep in the back seat, is hit in the chest and pronounced dead. A

Houston man's van explodes when he starts the ignition. Police say Lam Huu Diep, forty-four, became the city's first car-bombing fatality. Officers feel frustrated by their increasing inability to solve homicide cases. "Politicians won't commit adequate funding or resources to law enforcement," Officer Clark said, "and the justice system provides little deterrent."

We need to overhaul our justice system so that each offense carries the same punishment in every jurisdiction. Currently the crime of stealing might warrant a ten-year-or-more sentence in one state, or one city, but the very same crime might garner only probation in a neighboring district.

Many juveniles make the familiar claim that if they were to rob and murder a shopkeeper, all they would get as punishment is juvenile detention until they become twenty-one years old. Perhaps kids who commit murder should get a life sentence—the same as the eighteen-year-old who commits murder. If the only consequence for murdering another human being is a term in prison until the age of twenty-one, deterrence is nonexistent. Anyone old enough to murder another human being deliberately is old enough to serve the time, to face the reality of life in prison.

However, incarcerated youth in particular need rehabilitation programs, not just indefinite warehousing. Juvenile offenders need to learn marketable trades so when they get out, they have a chance at finding good-paying jobs. Psychological and substance abuse counseling while incarcerated gives these kids a chance at living productive lives. Now we just throw them in prison and forget them until they're released. We do not protect them once they are inside the walls, but we fear them when they come out, meaner, tougher, and more violent than when they went inside. Gerald Laney, a veteran of many years in prison who finally ended up on death row said, "everyone knows that prisons are the devil's playground, where only the strong survive."

U.S. Attorney General Janet Reno espouses a philosophy that could stem the tide of juvenile crime. She says, "We have to begin to look at children as a whole. It costs a lot more to send someone to prison than to make an investment up front." Noting that the nation needs more efforts aimed at reducing drug dependency, truancy, and domestic violence, Reno observed, "I've become convinced that the child that watches his father batter his mother comes to accept violence as a way of life." Reno pledged to bring federal agencies together in a united front to aid the states' crime-fighting efforts. After praising the work done so far, the nation's first female attorney general said that the next frontier should be providing more drug and alcohol treatment programs. "If these drug treatment programs can help us cut the recidivism rate, we can save money and lives."